time for reflection

the gift of friendship

When would you give these gifts?

Katie Kitching and Annie Sevier

Acknowledgements

The authors and publishers would like to thank the children at Buckland Infant School, Chessington, Kingston-upon-Thames, and Susannah Green and Maneesha Puri and their classes at Southfield Primary School, London W4, for their help and contributions during the preparation of this book. They would like to give special thanks to Roger Butler, R.E. Inspector, London Borough of Ealing, for his advice.

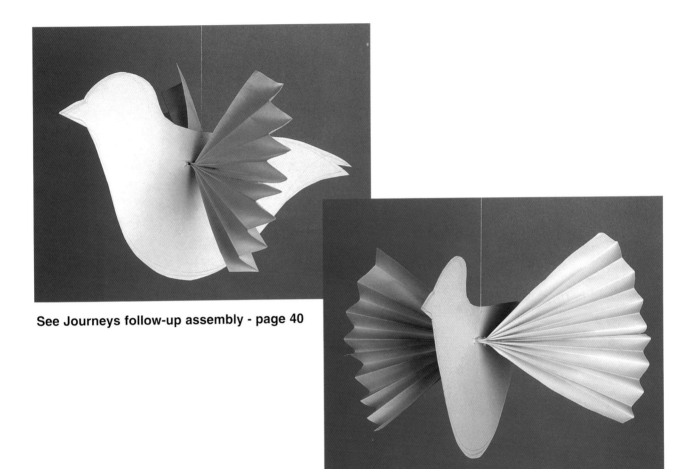

See Journeys follow-up assembly - page 40

First published in 1998 by BELAIR PUBLICATIONS LIMITED
Albert House, Apex Business Centre, Boscombe Road, Dunstable, LU5 4RL, United Kingdom.

© 1998 Katie Kitching and Annie Sevier
Reprinted 1999.

Series editor: Robyn Gordon
Photography: Kelvin Freeman

Design: Lynn Hooker
Line drawings: Glenn Goodwin

Printed in Hong Kong through World Print Limited

ISBN: 0 94788 274-X

Contents

Introduction 4

Artists 8
Autumn 9
Babies 10
Baskets 11
Bees and honey 12
Beginning the new school year 13
Bells 14
Bread 15
Candles 16
Caterpillars and butterflies 17
Changing 18
Christmas countdown 19
Christmas evergreens 20
Christmas - Simeon's story 21
Clothes 22
Colours 23
Divali 24
Doors 25
Easter 26
Eid-ul-Fitr 28
Families 29
Fishing 30
Flowers 31
Footsteps 32
Generosity 34
Gifts and giving 35
Guru Nanak's birthday 36
Hands 37
Helping 38
Homes 39

Journeys 40
Leaving 41
Loneliness 42
Music 43
Myself 44
Names 45
Neighbours 46
The New Year 47
Pancakes 48
Precious things 49
Promises 50
Remembering 51
St Francis 52
Seeing red and feeling blue 53
Sheep 54
Shoes 55
Spring 56
Stars 57
Sukkot 58
Summer 59
Sunshine 60
Thanksgiving 61
Toys 62
Vegetables 63
Water 64
Weaving 65
Why? 66
The wider world 67
Winter 68
Wishing and wanting 69

Follow-up Assemblies 70

THE ASSEMBLIES

- The assemblies in *Time for Reflection* have been specifically designed to capture children's interest and imagination. They also offer opportunities for sharing, celebrating and reflecting.
- Many of the assemblies focus on everyday childhood experiences and allow children to recognise their own hopes and fears, as well as those of others.
- Other assemblies link closely with classroom topics. In these assemblies there are opportunities to wonder at the world, explore moral issues and respond to the concerns of others.
- There are also assemblies that focus on particular religious festivals and the children are encouraged to respect the beliefs and customs of the different faiths.
- Throughout all the assemblies there is a strong emphasis on the use of visual stimuli and active pupil participation.
- There is a suggested act of worship to accompany each assembly.
- Each assembly can be adapted for the children to practise and present themselves.
- The assemblies can also be incorporated into class presentations.

N.B. Care must be taken if candles are used. These should be lit by an adult and kept at a safe distance from the children.

SUGGESTIONS FOR A GOOD CLASS PRESENTATION

Get the children to:

- keep each section short, and the whole assembly well paced.
- practise sections incidentally in class during the preceding weeks. Frequent but short practices develop familiarity and confidence without losing spontaneity.
- involve every child.
- give a warm welcome.
- capture the audience's interest by beginning with an assembly from this book.
- read and display a small selection of related topic work.
- recite a poem (individual or choral speaking).
- act out a short story wearing headbands, masks or hats. Use simple props and make sound effects with instruments.
- reflect on what has been said, and worship together.
- sing a song or hymn.
- thank everyone for coming.

Collect containers and fabrics for use in assemblies

VISUAL IMPACT

- Establish a visual focus for the assembly. A table with an adjacent screen is ideal.

- Use a range of different cloths to cover the table for different assemblies.

- Gather together the general equipment that will be used in the assemblies and store it in a suitable container. Useful items include:
    - scissors
    - felt-tip pens
    - strips of paper and card
    - a wall stapler
    - drawing pins
    - matches
    - wax tapers
    - a candle snuffer.

- Place the specific items needed for a particular assembly in a special container. The removal and disclosure of these special items heightens the children's anticipation and keeps them focused. Suitable containers include: baskets, boxes and bags.

- Use a rug or mat as a special place where a volunteer or helper could stand.

- Leave the specific items used in an assembly out on display to maintain the children's interest.

- Use appropriate gift wrap paper to add special interest to displays (see the Autumn assembly photograph on facing page).

- Add any follow-up work done by the children to the display.

Some ideas for seasonal candles

AMBIENCE AND ATMOSPHERE
- Create a calm atmosphere by being properly prepared yourself. Make sure you have everything ready before the children arrive.
- Play suitable music.
- Ensure the children enter the hall without speaking.
- Establish a consistent seating arrangement so that classes know where to sit and what is expected of them.
- Beckon or use other gestures to indicate what the children should do, and try to avoid talking yourself.
- Deal with any announcements, notices, etc., before the actual assembly starts.
- Signal the beginning of the assembly by lighting a candle. Vary the arrangement with the changing seasons.
- Establish a consistent dismissal procedure, again using gestures to signal which class should leave.
- Extinguish the candle and stop the music as the final child leaves the hall.

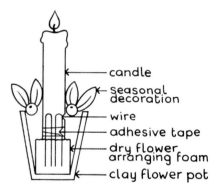

Replace the candle frequently to ensure that the candle flame never burns down close to the decorations.

MUSIC
- Select suitable music for the week.
- Ensure the children hear a variety of music from different cultures and times.
- Select a child to introduce the music at the beginning of the week. (If possible, let the child practise the reading in advance.)

SEATING
- Seat the classes in a U-shape if space permits. This allows you or the child helpers to walk around the central space showing items to the seated classes.
- Seat the youngest children nearest to the visual focus.

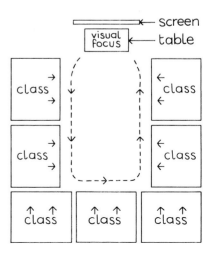

Collections for annual festivals, for example, Divali and Harvest

PUPIL PARTICIPATION

- Announce early on in the assembly that you will need volunteers or helpers, but do not select them until they are actually required. This will sustain interest in the assembly.
- In small schools, volunteers can be selected by putting all the children's names in a hat.
- In large schools, select the name or a class from a hat, and then invite volunteers from that particular class to help.
- Alternatively, you can select children from any class who have been listening attentively. This encourages good behaviour.

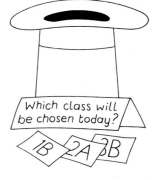

COLLECTIONS

- Store props that you have made for use in future years.
- Collect together pictures, artefacts and books that you will need for festivals that are celebrated each year. Make collections for:
    - Christmas
    - Divali
    - Easter
    - Eid-ul-Fitr
    - Harvest, etc.

- Keep a card index system and note down the stories, songs and poems that link with particular festivals or celebrations. Note the song book or poetry anthology where the selected texts can be found.

STORAGE

- Purchase stacking boxes for the collections in order to store items neatly, and for easy access.
- Store posters, pictures and gift wrap paper flat in an art portfolio.

Two apples and one lemon and four flowers. by David Hockney

Two real apples and one real lemon and four real Flowers by Aaron, Chantelle, Simon and Darminder

A suggested display for after the assembly

Focus: Artists help us to see the world in different ways.

You will need: a painting or reproduction of a still life that is easy to recreate using similar readily-available items, for example, 'Still Life with Fruit' by Vincent van Gogh, 'Pommes et Verre' by Paul Cezanne. Place all the items in a box.

The Assembly:
- Show the children the painting or reproduction.
- Tell the children the title of the picture and the name of the artist.
- Explain that you are going to select helpers to put out the things that the artist painted.
- Select volunteers to come up one-by-one and take an item from the box.
- Encourage them to place the items in the same positions as in the painting.
- Discuss how the children's re-creation matches the painting. What is the same? How is it different?

Reflection: Think about a picture you would like to paint. Close your eyes. Imagine how big the painting would be. Imagine what colours you would use.

Worship: Verse 1, 'Give to us eyes' from *Someone's Singing, Lord* (A&C Black).

Follow-up Assembly:
- This time select a portrait, for example, 'Self-Portrait' (1887) by Vincent van Gogh, 'Child with a Dove' by Pablo Picasso, or a painting combining a group of figures, for example, 'The Umbrellas' by Pierre-Auguste Renoir, 'Beach Scene' by Edgar Degas.
- Use hats, face paints, similar coloured garments or props to re-create the whole picture or just a part of it. For the suggested Picasso picture, make a paper dove (see Journeys follow-up assembly on page 40, and photograph on page 2).

AUTUMN

A suggested display for after the assembly

Focus: Autumn is a season of changes: changes in the growth of plants and in the behaviour of animals. These changes help them to survive the winter.

You will need: a bag containing a collection of seeds, fruits and leaves that fall from the trees in autumn, and a label for each item; if possible, a Canadian flag and a photograph of 'the fall'.

The Assembly:
- Ask the children if they know what season it is.
- Tell them that, in Canada, autumn is called "the fall". Ask them why they think this is.
- Show them the autumn bag.
- Take the autumn leaves out of the bag and ask why leaves fall in autumn.
- Choose some helpers to take each of the different fruits and seeds from the bag, and to show them.
- Select additional children to match the labels to the fruits and seeds.
- Discuss why fruits and seeds fall in autumn.
- Watch how the sycamore and lime seeds fall, then talk about seed dispersal.

Reflection: As the days get shorter and the weather gets colder, think about all the incredible changes that happen in nature.

Worship: Give thanks to God as you listen to this poem:
> Fall, leaves, fall; die, flowers, away;
> Lengthen night and shorten day;
> Every leaf speaks bliss to me
> Fluttering from the autumn tree.
>   Emily Brontë (1818-1848)

Follow-up Assembly:
- Demonstrate how to make a model hedgehog out of Plasticine and twigs.
- Invite some volunteers to make additional models.
- As they do this, talk about hibernation and the other ways in which animals prepare for winter.
- Talk about how some birds migrate.
- Discuss how the children can help those birds that stay behind by putting out suitable food.

BABIES

The display reads:
bib
bottle
nappies
sponge
rattle
cream
cotton buds
baby bath
baby lotion
baby boots
baby grow
blanket

A baby needs love.

Focus: Loving and caring.

You will need: a collection of items which a mother would use with a baby - bottle, nappy, changing mat, bib, rattle, etc., in a basket or bag; a large sheet of paper on a display board; and felt-tip pens.

The Assembly:
- Take the items out of the basket and discuss each in turn.
- How do parents care for their babies?
- Make a list of the things which a baby needs.
- What else does a baby need?
- Draw a heart round the list - a baby needs love and care.
- Who cares for a baby and gives it love? Talk about mothers, fathers, sisters, brothers and families.
- Jesus said that little children are important and that he loves little children.

Reflection: We all need love and care. Think about how God looks after us all like a loving father.

Worship: Golden slumbers kiss your eyes,
                  Smiles awake you when you rise,
                  Sleep little baby, do not cry,
                  And I will sing a lullaby.
                  God bless you.

                                    Thomas Dekker (1570-1641)

Follow-up Assembly:
- Compare and contrast babies with the children themselves: for example, what we can do now; what babies can and cannot do.
- Babies learn because somebody cares for them and loves them.
- Tell the children the story of Jesus and the children (Mark 10 : 13-16).

BASKETS

What is in the basket?

Focus: Life is full of surprises. You never know what you might find in a basket.

You will need: a Bible, a basket, a doll; three pieces of fabric - two plain, one patterned; a foil paper headband; jewels (if possible); and safety pins.

The Assembly:
- We are going to hear a story from the Bible about a sister who looked after her baby brother.
- Explain that the Bible is a book which is made up of many books, and in one of those books is the story of how the Hebrews once lived in a country called Egypt.
- Ask three girls to help - dress them by putting fabric round their shoulders - plain for Miriam and her mother, patterned for the princess who also wears the foil headband, and possibly some "jewels".
- Tell the story of the baby in the bulrushes (Exodus 2 : 1-10), asking the children to act out and illustrate the narrative.

Reflection: How do you think the mother felt leaving her baby?
How did Miriam feel when she saw the princess coming?
How do you think the princess felt when she found the baby?

Worship: The Lord bless thee and keep thee:
The Lord make his face to shine upon thee
and be gracious unto thee.
The Lord lift up his countenance upon thee
and give thee peace.
Numbers 6 : 24-26.

Follow-up Assembly:
- Tell the story of the loaves and the fishes (Mark 6 : 30-44).
- What was in the basket and how did Jesus use it?
- How do you think the boy felt when Jesus used his food to feed so many people?

BELLS

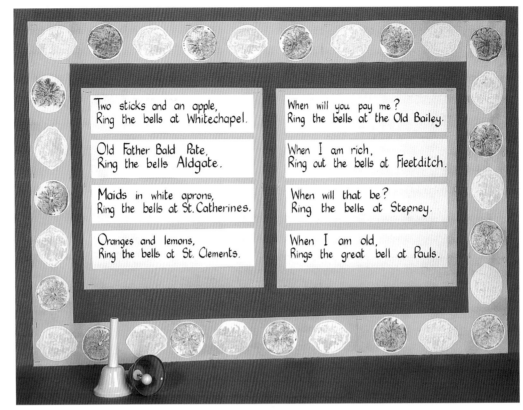

Two sticks and an apple,
Ring the bells at Whitechapel.

Old Father Bald Pate,
Ring the bells Aldgate.

Maids in white aprons,
Ring the bells at St. Catherines.

Oranges and lemons,
Ring the bells at St. Clements.

When will you pay me?
Ring the bells at the Old Bailey.

When I am rich,
Ring out the bells at Fleetditch.

When will that be?
Ring the bells at Stepney.

When I am old,
Rings the great bell at Pauls.

A suggested display for after the follow-up assembly

Focus: The sound of bells: celebrations and warnings.

You will need: a bell, a sheet of paper and some felt-tip pens. If possible, a variety of bells - a school bell, cow bells, a cat's collar with a bell, a set of hand bells, jingle bells, ankle bells; and a recording on tape or CD of church bells.

The Assembly:
- Ring a bell.
- How does the bell make its sound? Look at the shape, how it is held, what it is made from.
- Ask the children to think of different sorts of bells, and make a list of these.
- Discuss how some bells are used for joyful occasions, others for signalling danger. Can the children make suggestions for each kind of bell?
- Listen to the sounds made by the bells in the collection - describe the sounds.
- If you have a church bell recording, play this.

Reflection: Think of all the happy events that can be celebrated with bells.

Worship:　　　　If I had a bell, I'd ring it in the morning,
　　　　　　　　　　I'd ring it in the evening, all over this land,
　　　　　　　　　　I'd ring out a danger, I'd ring out a warning,
　　　　　　　　　　I'd ring out the love between my brother and my sister
　　　　　　　　　　All over this land.
　　　　　　　　　　　　　Third verse of 'If I had a hammer' in *Someone's Singing, Lord* (A&C Black)

Follow-up Assembly:
- Show the children a wedding card with a bell on it.
- Talk about church bells. How and when are they rung?
- Teach the children the 'Oranges and Lemons' song and game. (See words in the photograph above.)
- Choose eight children to demonstrate the game, and encourage the rest to join in the song.
- Play a recording of church bells if you can obtain this.

BASKETS

What is in the basket?

Focus: Life is full of surprises. You never know what you might find in a basket.

You will need: a Bible, a basket, a doll; three pieces of fabric - two plain, one patterned; a foil paper headband; jewels (if possible); and safety pins.

The Assembly:
- We are going to hear a story from the Bible about a sister who looked after her baby brother.
- Explain that the Bible is a book which is made up of many books, and in one of those books is the story of how the Hebrews once lived in a country called Egypt.
- Ask three girls to help - dress them by putting fabric round their shoulders - plain for Miriam and her mother, patterned for the princess who also wears the foil headband, and possibly some "jewels".
- Tell the story of the baby in the bulrushes (Exodus 2 : 1-10), asking the children to act out and illustrate the narrative.

Reflection: How do you think the mother felt leaving her baby?
                    How did Miriam feel when she saw the princess coming?
                    How do you think the princess felt when she found the baby?

Worship: The Lord bless thee and keep thee:
                    The Lord make his face to shine upon thee
                    and be gracious unto thee.
                    The Lord lift up his countenance upon thee
                    and give thee peace.
                                    Numbers 6 : 24-26.

Follow-up Assembly:
- Tell the story of the loaves and the fishes (Mark 6 : 30-44).
- What was in the basket and how did Jesus use it?
- How do you think the boy felt when Jesus used his food to feed so many people?

BEES AND HONEY

Focus: Busy bees - the amazing diversity of God's creations.

You will need: a large jar of honey, flower masks, bee headbands and bags of 'nectar'.

The Assembly:
* Show the children the jar of honey and talk about where it comes from.
* Explain that you and your actors are going to show how clever bees are, because even though they cannot talk, they have a special way of telling each other where the best flowers are.
* Seat the children wearing flower masks and carrying the bags of nectar at one end of the hall.
* Arrange the "bee" children at the other end of the hall - the hive area.
* Send the bees off to look for the flowers - remember only one bee finds the flowers.
* Call all the bees back to the hive area.
* Explain that the bee who found the flowers does a dance - the dancing bee performs a figure of eight dance, watched by the other bees.
* They all set off for the flowers, returning with the bags of nectar.

Reflection: Listen to a poem written by Isaac Watts nearly 300 years ago:

> How doth the little busy bee improve each shining hour
> And gather honey all the day from every opening flower!
> How skilfully she builds her cell, how neat she spreads the wax
> And labours hard to store it well, with the sweet food she makes.

Worship: We all enjoy honey. Thank you, God, for all the creatures of your world, big and small. Help us remember that even small creatures play a part in your creation.

Follow-up Assembly:
* Remind the children of how bees make honey.
* Tell the story of 'The Bee and Jupiter' (Aesop). Jupiter was so pleased with the gift of honey which the bee had given him that he promised to give her whatever she wanted. The spiteful bee asked for a sting which would destroy those she attacked. Jupiter gave her a sting but said that it would hurt her more than those she attacked, because she would have to leave it behind.

Focus: Making a good start to the school year.

You will need: a box containing a sandwich, a book and a plant in a pot; three separate lists written on card (1. bread, butter, filling; 2. paper, card, staples, ink; 3. seeds, soil, plant pot, water); a register for each class present; paper and felt-tip pens.

The Assembly:
• Explain that we are going to talk about beginnings.
• Show the children the first list - bread, butter, filling. Ask them what we will end up with if we begin with these things.
• Select a child to find and remove the sandwich from the box.
• Repeat for the other items.
• Now ask a child to hold up the class registers.
• Write a list of all the classes in the school.
• Discuss how we start this list at the beginning of the new school year. Together we make a school.
• Discuss with the children how we can make it a happy school.

Reflection: Think of the ways in which we all play a part in creating a happy school in which we learn together.

Worship: Dear God, help us to work and play together: each one of us being part of the whole.

Follow-up Assembly:
• Remind the children about the lists in the previous assembly.
• Talk about your own school rules and the reasons for having them.
• Ask the children for suggestions for class rules.
• Make a list of these.
• Ask the children to think of titles for their rules, such as 'Recipe for a happy day'.

BELLS

Two sticks and an apple,
Ring the bells at Whitechapel.

Old Father Bald Pate,
Ring the bells Aldgate.

Maids in white aprons,
Ring the bells at St. Catherines.

Oranges and lemons,
Ring the bells at St. Clements.

When will you pay me?
Ring the bells at the Old Bailey.

When I am rich,
Ring out the bells at Fleetditch.

When will that be?
Ring the bells at Stepney.

When I am old,
Rings the great bell at Pauls.

A suggested display for after the follow-up assembly

Focus: The sound of bells: celebrations and warnings.

You will need: a bell, a sheet of paper and some felt-tip pens. If possible, a variety of bells - a school bell, cow bells, a cat's collar with a bell, a set of hand bells, jingle bells, ankle bells; and a recording on tape or CD of church bells.

The Assembly:
- Ring a bell.
- How does the bell make its sound? Look at the shape, how it is held, what it is made from.
- Ask the children to think of different sorts of bells, and make a list of these.
- Discuss how some bells are used for joyful occasions, others for signalling danger. Can the children make suggestions for each kind of bell?
- Listen to the sounds made by the bells in the collection - describe the sounds.
- If you have a church bell recording, play this.

Reflection: Think of all the happy events that can be celebrated with bells.

Worship: If I had a bell, I'd ring it in the morning,
                   I'd ring it in the evening, all over this land,
                   I'd ring out a danger, I'd ring out a warning,
                   I'd ring out the love between my brother and my sister
                   All over this land.
                            Third verse of 'If I had a hammer' in *Someone's Singing, Lord* (A&C Black)

Follow-up Assembly:
- Show the children a wedding card with a bell on it.
- Talk about church bells. How and when are they rung?
- Teach the children the 'Oranges and Lemons' song and game. (See words in the photograph above.)
- Choose eight children to demonstrate the game, and encourage the rest to join in the song.
- Play a recording of church bells if you can obtain this.

BREAD

Focus: The importance of bread.

You will need: a selection of different kinds of bread in a basket - include some flat bread (pitta, chappati) and some matzo; if possible, yeast - either fresh or dried.

The Assembly:
- Many people think that bread is the most important kind of food there is. Why do you think this is?
- Look at the different sorts of bread in the basket. Invite children to help by taking the bread out of the basket and showing it to everyone. Talk about the shape, colour and size. Does anyone know why some bread is light and fluffy and some is flat?
- Explain to the children that some breads are not made with wheat flour.
- Explain, in simple terms, how yeast works.
- Tell the story of the first Passover (Pesach) when Jews had to leave Egypt in a great hurry, so there was no time for their bread to rise, and they made flat bread instead. Now Jews celebrate this every year by only eating flat unleavened bread for the eight days of the celebration of Pesach. Look at and taste matzos.

Reflection: There are some things which are so important that we must never forget them, even when they happened a long time ago.

Worship: (part of an ancient Jewish blessing)
> Blessed are you, O Lord our God, Eternal King,
> Who feeds the whole world with your goodness, with grace,
> with loving kindness and with tender mercy.

Follow-up Assembly:
- Remind the children of the story of Passover, and explain what happens in some Jewish households.
- Children could act this out: spring-cleaning the house, removing all traces of leavened bread, sweeping up any crumbs into a wooden tray with a feather (ready to be burned), and preparing the table for the special Passover meal.

CANDLES

I shall light a candle of understanding in your heart.

Focus: Jesus is the light of the world.

You will need: a collection of different sorts of candles, displayed safely on a table in suitable containers; two or three candle crowns; a wax taper and matches.

The Assembly:
- Talk about when we use candles. Ask the children for suggestions (birthdays, during power cuts, etc.).
- Talk about how Christians believe that Jesus is the light of the world, like a candle shining in the darkness.
- Light the candles.
- Tell the children that people often go into church to light a candle and have a quiet peaceful time during a busy day.
- Read the first verse of 'Jesus bids us shine' by Susan Warner (1819-1885).
- Explain that we are going to have a quiet time, watching our candles. Play some reflective music at this point.
- Choose children to wear the candle crowns. When the assembly is over, they will blow out the candles (under careful supervision, of course). If you have a candle snuffer, a child could use this.

Reflection: I shall light a candle of understanding in your heart, which shall not be put out.

(2 Esdras - 14:25)

Worship: Sing 'This little light of mine', *Alleluya* (A&C Black).

Follow-up Assembly:
Tell the children the following traditional story:
>   There was a king with two sons. He wanted to see which son was the wiser. He gave each a coin and told them to go out into the world and find something which would fill a large room. One son bought straw, but it was not enough to fill the room. The other son bought a candle. Why was this son wiser?

CATERPILLARS AND BUTTERFLIES

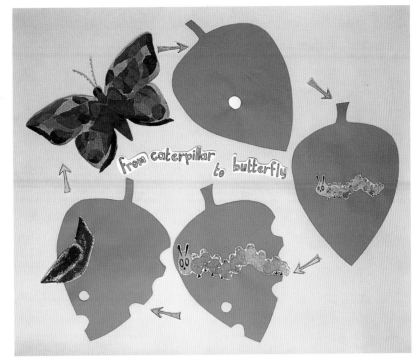

A suggested display for after the assembly

Focus: The wonder of change in nature.

You will need: *The Very Hungry Caterpillar* by Eric Carle (Picture Puffin); four pieces of green sugar paper cut into leaf shapes, about 40cm x 60cm; a piece of pink or blue sugar paper about 40cm x 60cm; scissors, felt-tip pens and safety pins.

The Assembly:
- Tell the story of *The Very Hungry Caterpillar.*
- Invite five children to help you.
- Draw an egg on a leaf shape - use a safety pin to attach the leaf to the back of the first child.
- Draw a small caterpillar on the next leaf, then pin the leaf to the back of the second child.
- Draw a larger caterpillar on the next leaf. If there is time, cut out some of the edge of the leaf to indicate that it has been eaten. Pin to the back of the third child.
- Draw a cocoon on the last leaf, pin this to the back of the fourth child.
- Using the blue/pink sugar paper folded in half, cut out a butterfly shape and pin this to the back of the fifth child.
- Arrange the children, first to fifth, in a line, facing the seated children.
- Turn round the first child - 'an egg on a leaf'; turn round the second child - 'hatches into a small caterpillar'; turn round the third child - 'the caterpillar eats and grows'; turn round the fourth child - 'it makes a cocoon'; turn round the fifth child - 'a beautiful butterfly comes out of the cocoon'.
- Make a circle of the five children and ask them to join hands and turn, illustrating the life cycle of the butterfly.

Reflection: Think about the wonderful things which happen in nature.

Worship: Thank you God for the wonders of your creation.

Follow-up Assembly:
You will need a packet of carrot seeds (emptied into a plain container), a scrubbed carrot concealed in another container, some peeled chopped carrot in a third container, and a blindfold. Empty the seeds into the palm of your hand and ask a volunteer to describe them. Blindfold the volunteer and give him/her the chopped carrot to taste and identify. Remove the blindfold and ask the child to show everyone the whole carrot. Contrast the tiny seeds with the fully grown carrot.

CHANGING

If you wear one of these crowns you have to face a special challenge! You have to try and change your behaviour! Some crowns are easier to wear than others. Which will you choose?

I will lend a help hand whenever I

I will share wha with others.

I will smile at everyone I me

ll listen carefu others.

I will take car th all my wor

take my turn pushing or ru

always tidy up I got out.

always rememb my chair in.

ill be polite veryone I meet

I will follow nstructions c

A suggested display for after the assembly

Focus: Some changes are easy to make, others are more difficult. Changing our behaviour is often quite a challenge, but it is possible.

You will need: some pre-prepared card crowns. Write a challenge on each crown, for example:
I will listen carefully to others.   *I will take my turn without pushing or rushing.*
Before the assembly, place the crowns in a line on two tables that have been pushed together.

The Assembly:
- Talk to the children about change.
- Ask two children to change places. Comment on how easy it is to change places.
- Talk about changing your mind. Ask the children for examples of when they have changed their minds. Find out whether it was easy or difficult.
- Discuss how changing our behaviour can be one of the most difficult things to do. At times we can all be untidy, bossy, careless, forgetful, selfish, bad-tempered, or even rude.
- Explain to the children about what the word 'challenge' means, and talk about the challenge crowns (see the sign in photograph).
- Select volunteers, one by one, to choose a crown to wear in their classrooms.

Reflection: Think about your own behaviour. What do you think needs to change? Imagine you are wearing one of the crowns, and try to meet the challenge for the rest of the day.

Worship:
Do all the good you can
By all the means you can
In all the ways you can
In all the places you can

At all the times you can
To all the people you can
As long as ever you can.

John Wesley (1703-1791)

Follow-up Assembly:
- Encourage each volunteer from the previous assembly to share his experience of wearing the challenge crown. Ask 'Which crown did you wear? Was it an easy or difficult thing to do? Why?'
- Tell the story of Zaccheus who completely changed his behaviour after meeting Jesus (Luke 19 : 2-8).
- Invite other children to wear the challenge crowns.

CHRISTMAS COUNTDOWN

Focus: Advent Sunday occurs on the fourth Sunday before Christmas Day. It marks the beginning of the Season of Advent - a time of expectation and hope.

You will need: four red and one white floating candles; a bowl of water; green food dye; a wax taper and matches; and a headband - on the front written: *1st December*. Draw holly leaves and berries on the headband, or get a child to decorate it with collage. (A further 24 headbands will be needed, one for each day in December leading up to Christmas.)

The Assembly
- Ideally, this assembly should take place on 1st December. However, if this is not possible, select the next convenient date.
- Ask the children what the date is, and why the beginning of December is such a special time.
- Tell them the story about the annunciation of Mary (Luke 1 : 26-38). (Mary was visited by the Angel Gabriel who told her that she was going to have a special baby, and that she was to call him Jesus.)
- Select a child to wear the headband. (If the assembly occurs after 1st December, select additional children to wear the subsequently dated headbands.)
- Explain that there will be a different headband for each day leading up to Christmas and that the children who wear them will be helping with the school's 'Countdown to Christmas'.
- Explain how in some churches a candle is lit on Advent Sunday and how an additional candle is lit every following Sunday, until the white candle is lit on Christmas day.
- Show the children the floating candles that have been bought for the school, and explain how you are going to make a special floating advent display.
- Select a volunteer to add the green dye to the water.
- Place one red candle on the water and light it.

Reflection: As Christmas gets nearer we shall see lots of lights - candles, stars, fairy lights on Christmas trees, maybe even Christmas lights in the streets. When you see them, remember it will soon be the birthday of Jesus.

Worship:

Light the candles on the tree
Christ was born for you and me.
Light the candles in the hall,
He was born to help us all.

Light the candles up and down,
In the country and the town.
Light the candles everywhere,
He was born a baby fair.

Christina G. Rosetti (1830-1894)

Follow-up Assembly: See page 70.

CHRISTMAS EVERGREENS

Focus: The scents and sounds of Christmas are brought together by a carol, a legend, and the making of a special seasonal pot pourri.

You will need: some sprigs of holly, ivy and rosemary (enough rosemary to allow for a sprig to be passed along each row of children); if possible, some sprigs of fir and laurel. Music: the carol, 'The Holly and the Ivy'.

The Assembly:
- Show the holly and ivy sprigs and see if the children can identify them.
- Ask the children to listen to the carol, 'The Holly and the Ivy'.
- Explain how long ago people thought it was lucky to have holly in the home, and how others thought ivy would keep them safe from illness (the plague).
- Find out if any of the children have holly in their homes at Christmas.
- Find out about which other plants or leaves they see at Christmas time.
- Tell, or ask a child to read, the final part of the Christmas story when Mary, Joseph and Jesus had to flee to Egypt (Matthew 2 : 13-15).
- Discuss why they had to travel by night. Explain how they probably had to cook, eat, sleep and wash outside.
- Tell the legend about how Mary washed the baby's clothes and placed them on a rosemary bush to dry.
- Show the sprigs of rosemary and then get the children to pass them along each row, smelling the sprig before handing it on to the next child.

Reflection: As you smell the rosemary, imagine how scared Mary and Joseph might have felt when they escaped. Remember that God protected them, and that God will look after you too.

Worship: Leave all your worries with God because he cares for you (1 Peter 5:7).

Follow-up Assembly: See page 70.

20

CHRISTMAS - SIMEON'S STORY

but Simeon kept on waiting........

Focus: The coming of the Messiah had long been predicted. Simeon knew that Jesus would come.

You will need: a puppet in three parts - a cross made of two pieces of thin wood, an oblong of cheese cloth, or similar fabric, with a hole in the centre, a head (made either from a cardboard cylinder or from dry flower arranging foam) depicting an old man. Put all the pieces in a bag, a basket or a box.

The Assembly:
- Explain that you are going to tell a story from the Bible and that in your bag/box/basket you have something which will help you to do this.
- Take out the wooden base of the puppet and hold it up. Ask the children if they have any ideas as to what it is.
- After a discussion, take out the cloth and drape it over the base, with the apex through the hole in the cloth. Do the children have any more ideas as to what it is?
- Finally, take out the head and complete the puppet.
- Tell the story of Simeon:

      There was once an old man called Simeon. He knew that a very special baby would be born.
      He knew this because he had read about it in the Old Testament of the Bible. Wise men called
      prophets had written about a saviour who would come to save them all (Luke 2 : 25-35).
      Simeon waited, and while he waited an angel came to tell Mary she would have a special baby.
      Simeon didn't know this - he just kept on waiting. Mary and Joseph went on their journey to
      Bethlehem, but Simeon didn't know this - he just kept on waiting. (Relate the Christmas story - the
      stable, the angels, the shepherds and the wise men: emphasising that Simeon didn't know that it
      was all happening, children joining in with "Simeon didn't know this, he just kept on waiting".)
      But when Jesus was six weeks old, he was taken to the temple by Mary and Joseph, and Simeon
      was there. As soon as he saw the baby he knew that his waiting was over.

Reflection: Imagine how Simeon must have felt when he saw the baby Jesus.

Worship: Sing a Christmas carol such as 'Away in a Manger', or you could play 'For unto us a Child is born' from Handel's 'Messiah'.

CLOTHES

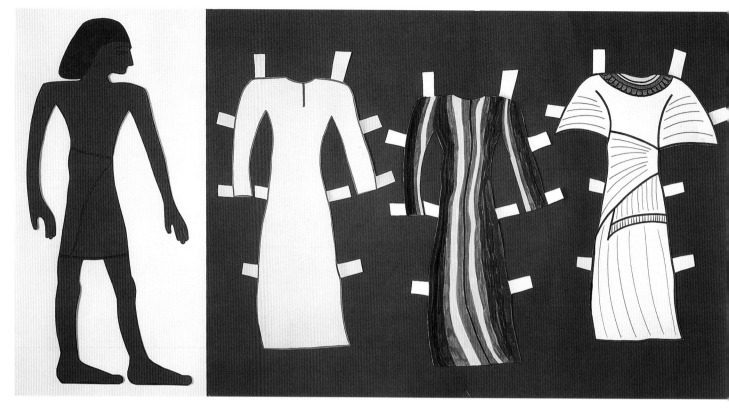

Focus: The story of Joseph, son of Jacob.

You will need: a cut-out cardboard mannequin of Joseph (approx 60cm tall) and two robes cut out of paper with flaps attached so that they fit over the mannequin (see photograph).

The Assembly:
- Show the children the Joseph figure and select a volunteer to 'dress' him in the drab robe.
- Tell the story of Joseph and his brothers (Genesis 37 : 3-35).
- Get another volunteer to change Joseph's clothes when the new robe is mentioned and to remove it when you reach the part of the story where he is thrown in the well.

Reflection: Think about what we can learn from this story. What do you think about Joseph? What do you think about his brothers?

Worship: Dear God, Joseph and his brothers did not always get along with each other. Sometimes we say things that upset others, just like Joseph did. Sometimes we get jealous just like his brothers did. Help us to get along with everyone.

Follow-up Assembly:
- Make a third robe out of white paper, drawing patterns to make it look like the garment of an ancient Egyptian.
- Tell the remainder of the story about how Joseph was eventually re-united with his father and brothers (Genesis 39 to 46 : 1-30). The bible text will need to be shortened and simplified.

COLOURS

A suggested display for after the assembly

Focus: Think of a world without any colour.

You will need: a table covered with a white cloth; a box of grey, black, white, metallic (silver) and transparent objects (there must be three containers amongst the transparent objects, for example, a tumbler, a vase, a bowl); a bottle of water; and food colouring - red, blue and yellow.

The Assembly:
- Explain that in the box there is a collection of objects which we are going to unpack.
- Ask individual children to remove an item from the box and place it on the table.
- When the display is complete, take a long look at it. What is missing?
- Pour water into the three transparent containers and add colour to each - red, blue and yellow.
- Discuss how colour adds beauty to our world.
- Read the poem 'What is pink' by Christina Rossetti (see below).

What is pink?

What is pink? A rose is pink
By the fountain's brink.
What is red? A poppy's red
In its barley bed.
What is blue? The sky is blue
Where the clouds float through.
What is white? A swan is white
Sailing in the light.

What is yellow? Pears are yellow,
Rich and ripe and mellow.
What is green? The grass is green,
With small flowers between.
What is violet? Clouds are violet
In the summer twilight.
What is orange? Why, an orange,
Just an orange!

Christina Rossetti

Reflection: Close your eyes and imagine that everything is grey. Now think of a rainbow.

Worship:

You, whose day it is,
make it beautiful.

Get out your rainbow colours
so it will be beautiful.

Nootka Sing

Follow-up Assembly:
Read *Elmer the Patchwork Elephant* by David McKee (Red Fox), the story of a colourful elephant who wanted to be grey.

DIVALI

Focus: At Divali, many Hindu families hope that the goddess Lakshmi will visit their homes and bless them with prosperity and good fortune.

You will need: two tables - cover one with a beautiful brightly coloured cloth; on the other place a box containing a picture or statue of Lakshmi, a small vase of flowers, a bowl of fresh fruit, a bowl of water, a bell, some incense sticks in a holder and some divas (or night-lights) on a tray, a wax taper and matches.

The Assembly
- Begin by telling the children that you are going to show them a picture of a very special Hindu goddess.
- Tell them that you have put the beautiful cloth on the table because that is where the picture is going to be.
- Take the picture from the box and show it to the children, telling them the name of the goddess Lakshmi. Explain that because Lakshmi is very special, many Hindu families will put special things in front of her (flowers, fruit, water, incense, a bell, and some divas).
- Select children to do this.
- Light an incense stick. Explain that this is a special time for those Hindu families because they hope Lakshmi will visit their homes and bless them. Explain how homes are cleaned ready for her arrival; how patterns are painted on the floor to welcome her; and how small lamps are placed on window sills and outside doors to attract her attention.
- Now light the divas.

Reflection: Think about your family and all the good things that you would like them to have.

Worship:

As you see the diva lights burning bright,
Perhaps you can imagine Lakshmi visiting at night.
Happy Divali to everyone here.
May everyone have a good new year.

Say to the children, 'Turn to the person sitting next to you. Wish each other "Happy Divali"'.

Follow-up Assembly: See page 70.

DOORS

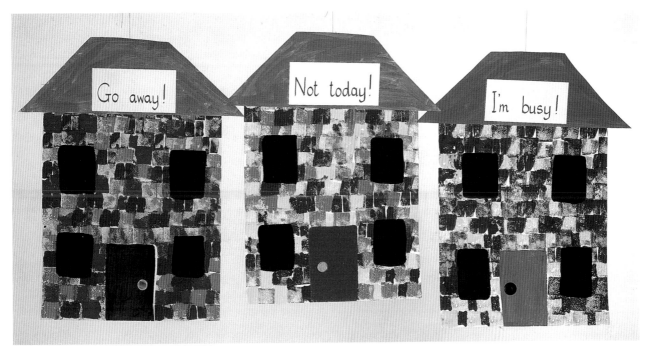

Focus: Welcoming and being friendly towards all the people we meet.

You will need: three large doors, made from card; a sketch of your own school doors; a visitor's badge. (Your helpers will need to be briefed as to their responses.)

The Assembly:
- Ask four children to help you. Give three children the 'doors' to hold.
- The fourth child pretends to knock on the first door and receives the response 'Go away!' The second door: 'Not today!' The third door: 'I'm busy!'
- Ask the child how it feels to be sent away. Discuss this with the children.
- Show everyone the sketch of your school doors. Ask them where they see these doors.
- If you were a visitor coming through the doors, what would you hope to find?
- Explain that visitors to the school are asked to wear badges, and show them the example of your badge.

Reflection: Think about our school. Do we make people welcome?

Worship: Dear God, help us to give a warm welcome to visitors who come to our school.

Sing: 'How do you do', in *Games Songs with Prof. Dogg* (A&C Black).

Follow-up Assembly
- Pre-prepare a garland of tissue paper flowers.
- Begin the assembly by showing the garland. Demonstrate how to make an individual flower and discuss how to thread the flowers together.
- Explain that in some countries (India, the Pacific Islands) garlands are placed around a visitor's neck as a special welcome.
- Place some garlands round volunteers' necks.
- Talk about other ways we can welcome or greet people.

EASTER

Focus: The triumphant welcome of Jesus to Jerusalem, and the events leading up to his death.

You will need: a sheet of green sugar paper, adhesive tape, scissors, a Bible and a palm cross; if possible, a model donkey and a book about Jerusalem.

The Assembly:
- Roll up the paper loosely. Make cuts as shown, then pull from the centre to make the palm branch and secure the 'stem' with adhesive tape.
- Tell the children the story of Palm Sunday (Matthew 2l : 1-11).
- Explain how Christians go to church on Palm Sunday to remember the day that Jesus came to Jerusalem.
- Show the palm cross.
- Explain that these are given to the people who are in church on Palm Sunday.

(For a class assembly, make additional palm fronds and get the children to act out the story.)

Reflection: Think about why Jesus was a special person.

Worship: Sing 'Hurrah for Jesus' in *Someone's Singing, Lord* (A&C Black).

Follow-up Assembly:
- Tell the children a simplified version of the events leading up to the death of Jesus (Mark 14 : 1-2 and 10-72, and 15 : 1-37).
- Discuss how this is a very sad time for Christians.
- Show a hot cross bun and ask the children why these are eaten at Easter time.
- End the assembly by saying that although today's story has been very sad, Christians believe it has a happy ending which you will tell them about next time.

EASTER

A suggested display for after the follow-up Assembly - see page 70

Focus: The Christian belief in the resurrection of Jesus.

You will need: a crucifix; six square pieces of white paper (20cm x 20cm); and some coloured felt-tip pens.

The Assembly:
- Explain that you are going to make a display after the assembly and that you will need six volunteers to begin the artwork during the assembly.
- Show the paper and pens.
- Explain that you are going to ask each one of them to draw a different part of the assembly story.
- Show all the children the crucifix and remind them about how sad the followers of Jesus felt on the Friday he died.
- Explain how the body of Jesus was put in a safe place - in a tomb with a huge rock across the entrance (Matthew 27 : 57-60).
- Tell the children what happened after this. As you tell each part of the story, select a volunteer to come and draw what happened.
  - The discovery of the empty tomb (John 20 : 1-10)
  - Jesus appears to Mary Magdalene (John 20 : 11-18)
  - The walk to Emmaus (Luke 24 : 13-31)
  - Jesus appears to his disciples (John 20 : 19-22)
  - Jesus and Thomas (John 20 : 19 - 22)
  - Jesus appears to his disciples out fishing (John 2l : 1-13).
- Explain that, for Christians, Easter means new life and hope. It shows that God cares.
- For the display, arrange the pictures in the shape of a cross, and use strips of wrapping paper (spring flower design) as borders (see line drawing).

Reflection: Close your eyes. Imagine an Easter egg. Think about all the other signs of new life at Easter.

Worship: Sing 'Morning has broken' in *Someone's Singing, Lord* (A&C Black).

Follow-up Assembly: see page 70.

EID-UL-FITR

Focus: Eid-ul-Fitr marks the end of Ramadan, the month of fasting. It is a happy celebration for Muslim families.

You will need: a sunrise/sunset model (see page 70); identically-sized silver and black paper circles; some dates; a banner reading 'Eid Mubarak'; if possible, some Eid cards and a model of a mosque (attach an outline drawing of a mosque to a box).

The Assembly:
- Ideally this assembly will take place as soon as possible after Eid-ul-Fitr.
- Overlap the black and silver circles to create a new crescent moon (see photograph). Ask the children what they think it is.
- Explain that when Muslim families saw the moon looking like this, one month ago, they knew it was time for Ramadan (the month of fasting) to begin.
- Using the sunrise/sunset model, explain that, during Ramadan, Muslims should not eat or drink between sunrise and sunset.
- Invite some children to sample the dates, explaining that these are usually the first food Muslims eat when breaking the fast at sunset.
- Select a volunteer to create a new crescent moon. Explain that this new moon signals the end of Ramadan. It means that fasting can end. It is now Eid-ul-Fitr - a time of celebration.
- Talk about what happens at Eid-ul-Fitr:
    - how Muslims wear new clothes for Eid
    - how they go to the mosque to pray (if possible, show model)
    - how they visit family and friends, taking sweets and cakes
    - how they exchange cards (if possible, show cards)
    - how they share a special meal
    - how they give to the poor.
- Select two volunteers to hold up the banner and teach the children how to say the traditional greeting 'Eid Mubarak'.

Reflection: A Muslim greeting is 'As-salaamu wa alaykum'. It means 'Peace be with you'. The reply is 'Wa alaykumu-s-salaam', which means 'And upon you be peace'.

Worship: May peace be with everyone here today. (It would not be appropriate to end with 'Amen'.)

Follow-up Assembly: See page 70.

FAMILIES

The family charts shown read:

me	my close family who live with me	my wider family
Titch	mum dad Pete Mary baby	

me	my close family who live with me	my wider family
Leon	mummy Lorella	granny grandad 1 uncle 3 aunties 4 cousins great gran

We are all part of God's family.

Focus: The importance of families.

You will need: a collection of books concerning families, for example, 'Titch' books, by Pat Hutchins; 'The Large Family' books by Jill Murphy; 'Mog' books by Judith Kerr; two family charts (see photograph); if possible, a reproduction of Millais' painting 'Jesus in the house of his parents' (Tate Gallery, London).

The Assembly:
- Discuss the books you have selected. Ask the children who is in each of the families.
- Fill out a family chart for Titch (there will be no entry in the wider family column).
- Ask the children to think about their own families, then select a child to fill out (with your help) a second family chart for his/her own family.
- Draw the children's attention to the fact that some children have small close families and others have large extended ones. Families come in all sizes.
- Explain that Jesus lived with his family for a long time before he began his important work: his father Joseph was a carpenter and Jesus might have helped him in his workshop.
- Show the children the reproduction of the Millais painting if you have it.
- Sing 'How many people', from *Tinderbox* (A&C Black).

Reflection: Families come in many sizes, some big, some small. Remember that we are all part of God's family.

Worship: God bless all those that I love;
God bless all those that love me:
God bless all those that love those that I love
And all those that love those that love me.

                                A prayer from New England

Follow-up Assembly:
- Discuss families - think about things which families do together. Write a list of children's examples (for example, eating, shopping, swimming).
- What do you think Jesus might have done with his family?

FISHING

A suggested display for after the assembly

Focus: The followers of Jesus who became "fishers of men".

You will need: a Bible, crêpe paper; scissors, a piece of A4 card and a felt-tip pen; if possible, a toy boat and some fishing net to go on the assembly table.

The Assembly:
- If you know there are children present with the names Simon, James and John, call them out to the front (or choose three volunteers from the group) - and at the same time begin to cut the crêpe paper to make a net. (See line drawing below.)
- Jesus had friends who helped him and followed him - but they had jobs before they met him. Explain to the children that you are making something which will help them guess what the jobs were.
- Cut the crêpe paper and unfold the net. 'What did Jesus' friends do when he first met them?' Ask the volunteers to weave the foil fish into the net.
- Show the children the Bible, and explain that there is a story in one of its books which tells how Jesus helped his fishermen friends.
- Tell the story of the great catch of fish (Luke 5: 4-10), and ask the volunteers to act it out.
- Draw a fish on the piece of card and explain that Christians use this as a sign to remind them of Jesus (see photograph).
- The fishermen left their boats and followed Jesus - they became 'fishers of men'. This means they told others about Jesus.

Reflection: How do you think the fishermen felt when they caught so many fish? Why did they give up their work? Why did they follow Jesus?

Worship: Sing 'Now Jesus one day' from *Someone's Singing, Lord* (A&C Black).

Follow-up Assembly:
- Remind the children of the Christian sign of the fish.
- Introduce the word 'disciple'. Explain its meaning and tell how Jesus had twelve disciples who followed him and helped him.
- Retell the story from John 21: 1-14, in which Jesus appeared to the disciples after The Resurrection.

FLOWERS

the queen of Sheba

king Solomon

Can you tell which are the real flowers?

Focus: Flowers come in a great variety of different forms. All are very beautiful.

You will need: two flower stems of the same species (one real and the other artificial) in two vases (cover these with an upturned box); two cylinder heads (one for King Solomon and the other for the Queen of Sheba).

The Assembly:
- Begin by introducing King Solomon. Explain how God had asked him what he wanted and how the king had asked for wisdom (1 Kings 3 : 5-14).
- Tell the children how God had indeed made him very, very wise.
- Introduce the Queen of Sheba. Recount how she went to visit King Solomon to find out if he really was as wise as people said (1 Kings 10 : 1-3).
- Now tell the legend about one of the tests she gave him: She had some flowers made that looked exactly like real flowers. She asked the king to tell her which the real flowers were, but she said he could not touch nor smell them.
- At this point, lift the box to reveal the flowers, and set the children the same task. (They should remain seated.)
- As the children make guesses, ask them for their reasons and how they think King Solomon solved the problem. *(He asked his servant to place the flowers by an open window. A bee flew in and eventually settled on the real flowers to collect nectar.)*

Reflection: Think about a flower that you really like. Why is it your favourite? Close your eyes and try to imagine it.

Worship: Listen to the words of Jesus:
> 'Look how the wild flowers grow: They do not work or make clothes for themselves.
> But I tell you not even King Solomon with all his wealth had clothes as beautiful as one of
> these flowers.'   (from the Sermon on the Mount, Matthew 6 : 28-29)

Follow-up Assembly:
- You will need a mixed bunch of flowers wrapped in paper, and a vase filled with water.
- Unwrap the flowers and place them on a table.
- Invite a child to select a flower and say why s/he likes it before placing it in the vase.
- Repeat until the vase is full and the flower arrangement complete.

FOOTSTEPS

Note: Tracks are not to scale.
© Belair (copiable page)

FOOTSTEPS

The 12 disciples - see follow-up assembly

Focus: Following in the footsteps of others.

You will need: an overhead projector; a transparency of the animal and bird tracks (photocopy page 32 on to an OHP transparency sheet); a shallow tray of damp sand; and a blindfold.

The Assembly:
- Begin the assembly by looking at the OHP transparency (photocopied from facing page).
- Find out if the children can identify any of the tracks.

Key to OHP transparency:	1. duck	2. cow
	3. dog	4. crow
	5. rat	6. cat

- Now ask for four volunteers. Explain that one will be blindfolded, then one of the remaining three will be silently beckoned forward to make a footprint in the damp sand.
- When completed, remove the blindfold and ask the child which of the others made the footprint. Ask the child to explain how the decision was reached.
- Discuss what it means 'to follow in someone's footsteps'.
- Suggest ways in which the children can follow the good examples of others. See what suggestions the children have.

Reflection: Think of someone you know who is always kind and helpful. Think about how you can copy their behaviour - how you can follow in their footsteps.

Worship: Day by day, dear Lord, of thee
                     three things I pray:
                     to see thee more clearly,
                     love thee more dearly,
                     follow thee more nearly,
                     day by day.   Richard of Chichester (1197 - 1253)

Follow-up Assembly:
- You will need the names of the 12 disciples written on cards (one per card).
- Tell the children that Jesus had lots of followers and find out if they know the name given to his 12 special followers.
- Also find out if they know any of the disciples' individual names (see photograph above).
- Ask volunteers to hold up the 12 name cards and read them together.
- Explain how the disciples listened to Jesus teaching and how they helped him.
- Tell the story of the loaves and the fishes (Mark 6 : 30-44).

GENEROSITY

Focus: God forgives us. He is generous.

You will need: fifteen large circular coins made from foil, in a bag or basket; a Bible; five demonstration clocks; and grapes.

The Assembly:
- Ask a group of children (about sixteen in all) to help you.
- Explain that you are going to tell a story from the Bible. It is a story that Jesus told (Matthew 20 : 1-16).
- Explain that Jesus told many stories which had a meaning. Often the meaning was hidden and people had to really think hard in order to understand. This story is about a man who owned a vineyard.
- Choose a child to be the owner of the vineyard.
- Show the children the grapes. Explain that the workers would have been picking grapes and that this was hard work, especially as the weather would have been hot.
- Tell the story of the workers in the vineyard, using the children as the characters. Use the demonstration clocks to show the times.
- Ask the 'vineyard owner' to pay the 'workers' - of course, all get the same amount of money.
- Is it fair that all the workers get the same amount, despite how long they worked? Ask for comments.
- Explain that Jesus meant to show the people that God gives equally to all, and that we should not be jealous because we think we have done more than others. God is generous to all.

Reflection: Help us to give freely and be generous, as God is generous.

Worship: Sing 'Magic Penny', *Alleluya* (A&C Black).

> Thank you, God, for your forgiveness: help me to understand your word.

Follow-up Assembly:
Tell another story that Jesus told about generosity and forgiveness: the Prodigal Son (Luke 15 : 11-32).

GIFTS AND GIVING

Focus: There are special times when we give gifts, but the gift of friendship can be given every day.

You will need: a piece of card cut into a heart shape on which is written - 'the gift of friendship'. Place this inside a plain box which is then gift-wrapped.

The Assembly:
• Ask the children to think about the Christmas story and to tell you what gifts were given to Jesus when he was born.
• Show them the special gift-wrapped box. Ask them who it might be for and what might be inside it.
• Having got a number of suggestions and stimulated the children's curiosity, open up 'the gift'.
• Feign disappointment that there is nothing inside. Turn the box upside down to prove it is empty, but let the heart fall out as you do so.
• Select a child to pick up the heart and to read the words on it.

Reflection: What does it mean? How can you give a gift of friendship? Is it something you only give on special occasions, or is it something you can give every day?

Worship: More and more for Jesus
May we gladly give
Giving, giving, giving
Is the way to live.
Julia H. Johnson (1849-1919)

Follow-up Assembly:
• Using a range of different wrapping papers (birthday, wedding, new baby, Mother's Day, Silver Wedding, Easter, etc.), gift-wrap a variety of boxes. Ask the children to think what might be inside each one, who they might give them to, and on what special occasion.
• End the assembly with the reminder that the gift of friendship is something that can be given every day.

GURU NANAK'S BIRTHDAY

How can you tell that Guru Nanak was a very special person?

Focus: Guru Nanak was the founder of the Sikh religion. His birthday is celebrated in late autumn/early winter. (The precise date varies from year to year, so check a festivals calendar or education diary for details.)

You will need: a picture of Guru Nanak and two other portraits (exclude religious figures or saints from your selection); and a table covered with a special cloth. Place the pictures in a bag or box before the assembly so that the children cannot see them.

The Assembly:
- Select three volunteers to come up and stand facing the seated children.
- Give each one a portrait to hold, making sure that only they, and not the seated children, can see their pictures. Ask each volunteer to describe the person in the picture.
- Now get the volunteers to show the pictures to all the children. Find out if they notice anything else. Do they think there is anything special about one of the portraits?
- Discuss the halo of light shining around Guru Nanak, and what halos signify.
- Tell the children that Guru Nanak was a very special holy man who lived about 500 years ago.
- Tell them when his birthday is celebrated and place his picture on the table which is covered in the special cloth.

Reflection: Guru Nanak taught people to love God, to care for each other and to work hard. Think about why these were such wise words.

Worship: Listen carefully as I read these words taken from the Sikh's holy book - the Guru Granth Sahib.

> Just as there is scent in a flower
> And a reflection in a mirror,
> So God is in you.
> Find him in your heart.   (It would not be appropriate to end with 'Amen'.)

Follow-up Assembly: See page 70.

HANDS

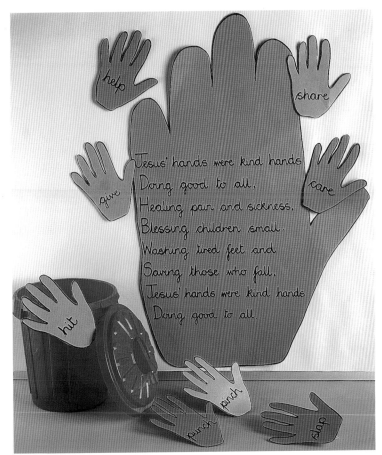

Focus: Helping hands.

You will need: the first verse of 'Jesus' hands were kind hands' written on a large piece of card shaped like a hand; eight small card hands on each of which is written one of the following words: *help, care, share, give, hit, pinch, slap, punch;* and a small plastic dustbin or a wastebin.

The Assembly:
- Give out the eight small hands to eight volunteers.
- Sing 'Jesus' hands were kind hands', in *Someone's Singing, Lord* (A&C Black).
- Ask each child, in turn, what is written on their cardboard hand, and discuss whether their hand is a *helping* hand or a *hurting* hand.
- Pin the helping hands on the display, round the large hand, and discard the hurting hands into the bin.

Reflection: Let us look at our hands, and think about how they can be helpful hands.

Worship: My hands can help, my hands can share,
My hands can give, my hands can care.
Dear Jesus - make my hands helping hands,
Make my hands sharing hands,
Make my hands giving hands,
Make my hands caring hands.
Make my hands gentle hands so that I may grow
More like you every day.

Follow-up Assembly:
- Display a collection of protective gloves, for example, oven gloves, gardening gloves, surgical gloves, household gloves.
- Explain how we can use our hands for doing lots of useful things, but that sometimes our hands need special protection. Discuss why and when people wear protective gloves.

HELPING

How can we help the little red hen?

Focus: Many hands make light work.

You will need: a bag of wheat grains, a spade, a hoe, a rake and a watering can (these can be full-size, or from a toy set). If possible, have a scythe and two flat stones. If it is a class assembly, the children could give a small loaf of bread to each class at the end of the assembly (loaves either made by children or bought).

The Assembly:
- Talk about the tools and how they are used.
- Tell the story of the Little Red Hen and the grains of wheat, using children to act the parts of the characters.
- When the story is finished, discuss the way each character behaved and whether this was fair.
- Retell the story, this time each character helping in some way.
- Ask each child to explain how he or she is going to help the Little Red Hen. For example,
    'I have a spade, I will dig.'
    'I have a rake, I will make the ground smooth', and so on.

Reflection: Think about how we can help each other and share responsibility.

Worship:

    The things good Lord, that we pray for,
    Give us grace to work for,
    through Jesus Christ our Lord.

                    Sir Thomas More (1478-1535)

Follow-up Assembly:
- Have ready four badges, labelled: *caretaker, cleaner, mid-day supervisor, secretary.* (Before the assembly, ask the caretaker, cleaner, mid-day supervisor and secretary to suggest three ways in which the children could help them. Write these as a list.)
- Remind the children about how we should help.
- Ask four children to help you. Give each a badge.
- How can we help each of these people? Check against the lists given by the staff involved.

HOMES

Headbands - clockwise from top - tree, moth, mouse, wasp, bird and woodlouse

Focus: There is no place like home.

You will need: The headbands and props shown in the photograph above. If you are producing a class assembly you should have more than one of each creature so that all the class can be involved.

The Assembly:
- Select seven volunteers.
- Equip the creatures with their headbands (mouse, bird, moth, wasp and woodlouse). Give the woodcutter the axe, and the tree its leafy headband and branches.
- Get the tree character to stand in a central position.
- The woodcutter begins the story by saying 'I am going to cut down the tree'.
- Get the creatures to introduce themselves one by one.

> 'I am a - mouse/bird/moth/wasp/woodlouse.
> I live - in the roots/in the branches/in a gall/on a twig/in the trunk/under the fallen leaves.
> If the trees gets cut down, where will I live?
> I am so small and weak I can't do anything.'

- Now the tree surprises everyone by talking, and says:

> 'Each one of you may be small and weak, but together I am sure you can do something to save me and your homes.'

- The creatures think about what the tree has said, then each one explains how they can try to keep the woodcutter away.

> 'I can stop him cutting down the tree by - nibbling his nose/pecking his arms/fluttering in his face/stinging his hands/tickling his legs.'

- As the woodcutter approaches the tree s/he is chased away by all the creatures.
- End with the tree saying 'thank you'.

Reflection: Think about your home. Think about who lives there. Think about why your home is a special place.

Worship: Sing 'A house is a house for me' in *Tinderbox* (A&C Black).

Follow-up Assembly: See page 71.

Focus: Keeping in touch with family and friends.

You will need: assorted musical instruments; the book *A Balloon for Grandad* by Nigel Gray (pub. Oliver & Boyd); if possible, a red helium balloon (or a red balloon on a garden cane).
(As a class assembly, it will need to be rehearsed.)

The Assembly:
- Talk about being parted from family and friends (there may be children who have family members living far away).
- Explain that although we may be far apart, we still think of these family members and friends.
- Read, or tell, the story of the red balloon: Sam lets go of his balloon and it drifts away in the wind. His father tells him that the balloon will travel across the mountains, the sea and the desert until it reaches his grandfather, who will be glad to know that Sam is thinking of him.
- Use musical instruments to illustrate, in sound, the mountains, the sea, the desert - a child could show the balloon's journey as the story unfolds, using the balloon.

(As a class assembly, group paintings and collage of the scenery could have been prepared.)

Reflection: Even if we are far apart, we can still make a journey to people we love by thinking about them.

Worship: May the road rise to meet you.
           May the wind be also at your back.
           May the sun shine warm upon your face.
           May the rains fall softly upon your fields.
           Until we meet again,
           May God hold you in the hollow of his hand.
                                        Traditional Irish blessing

Follow-up Assembly:
(You will need: a bird shape, and paper to fold for wings.)
- Explain that many years ago there was no post, and messages were sent by carrier pigeon.
- Tell the children how this was done.
- Make the bird by folding (pleating) the wing paper and slotting it through the bird shape (see photograph on page 2).
- If you could send a message, to whom would you send it, and what would you say?

LEAVING

Focus: The finish of a school year and the farewells that this brings.

You will need: happy and sad puppets - one for each child (or one which they can pass between them).

The Assembly:
- Discuss how some children will soon be leaving to go to a new school. Everyone else will go to a new class.
- Select at least one volunteer from each class to hold the reversible puppet(s).
- Begin with the sad face(s). Ask each child to give a reason why s/he feels sad about leaving her/his present class/school.
- Ask the children to turn the puppet(s) round to show the happy face(s) and discuss what they are looking forward to in their new classes, or school, next term.
- Read the following poem.

> Goodbye to the old
> Hello to the new,
> I'll always remember
> Friends like you.
>
> In new places
> With new faces,
> I think it is true
> That I am who I am
> Because I knew you.

Reflection: It is sad to leave things and places and people we know well, but it is time for new beginnings and this should make us happy.

Worship:
> God be in my head, and in my understanding,
> God be in my eyes, and in my looking
> God be in my mouth and in my speaking
> God be in my heart and in my thinking.
>
> from The Book of Hours (1514)

LONELINESS

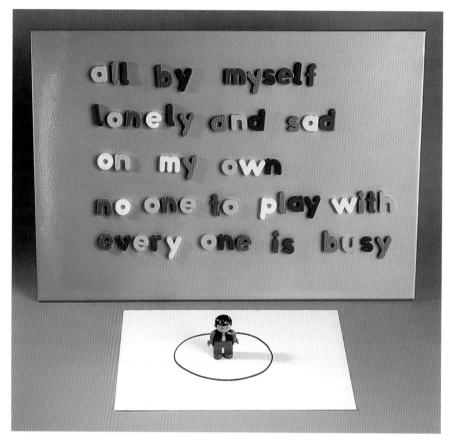

Focus: The difference between being alone and being lonely.

You will need: five pieces of A4 card; a felt-tip pen; a magnet board and magnetic alphabet letters; a small model figure; and a sheet of paper.

The Assembly:
- Begin by talking about being alone. What does this mean? Is it always a bad thing? Explain that sometimes we like to be by ourselves, and compare this with times when we do not like to be alone.
- Write the letters **a, l, o, n, e** on the pieces of card, and ask five children to help you by holding them in order to spell 'alone'.
- Now use the magnetic board and letters to make the acrostic. (Sort out the letters you will need beforehand.)

> **a** ll by myself
> **l** onely and sad
> **o** n my own
> **n** o one to play with
> **e** veryone is busy

- Draw a circle on the piece of paper and place the figure inside it. Is this how it feels when you are lonely? Ask the children for ideas of what we can do if someone is all alone.

Reflection: Sometimes it is good to be alone, but not always. Think about how we can be kind to people who might be lonely.

Worship: 'Look out for loneliness' (verse one) in *Someone's Singing, Lord* (A&C Black), or 'When I needed a neighbour' in *Someone's Singing, Lord.*

Follow-up Assembly:
- Tell the story of Jesus' time in the wilderness (Matthew 4 : 1-11).
- Ask the children if they can describe how Jesus must have felt.

MUSIC

A suggested display for after the assembly

Focus: The central part that music plays in many cultures.

You will need: a tape or CD of Japanese music; a shallow tray half-full of clean, dry cat litter; some large pebbles; a cardboard comb (see photograph); a bag containing a selection of Japanese artefacts, books and prints of Japanese life (past and present).

Suggestion: Before the assembly, calculate how many volunteers you will need to show the items from the bag, and select an additional volunteer to help with the demonstration.

The Assembly:
- Tell the children that in today's assembly they are going to be doing a lot of listening and looking, and that neither you nor they will be doing any talking until the end of the assembly.
- Select the required number of volunteers, seat them at the front and tell them that they will each hold up something when you quietly beckon them.
- Start the music and listen for 1-2 minutes without any action.
- Now beckon the volunteers, one by one, to show the items from the bag as the music continues to play.
- Beckon the final volunteer and demonstrate how to make patterns in the 'gravel' in the miniature Zen garden using the cardboard comb.
- Finally, let the music play for a further 1-2 minutes without any activity.

Reflection: Ask the children to sit quietly in silence for a few moments and think about all the things they have seen, and about the music that has been playing.

Worship: Sing 'Music of the World a-turnin', in *Alleluya* (A&C Black).

Assembly Ending: Ask the children if they enjoyed the music and if they know which country it came from. Discuss the things they saw, and explain that some real Japanese temple gardens do not have any plants in them, only gravel and stones. If possible, arrange for the children to file past the miniature Zen garden as they leave the hall.

Follow-up Assembly: See page 71.

Focus: We are all special.

You will need: a large shoe box with a lid (decorated on the outside, and with a lightweight mirror glued firmly in the base of the box); paper and felt-tip pens; a hat or bag containing all the class names.

The Assembly:
- Show the children the box - and ask them to guess what is in it.
- Explain that inside the box there is something very special and very precious, and that in fact there is only one of its kind in the whole world.
- Discuss with the children what this could be.
- Make a list of the ideas which come from your discussion.
- Explain that you are going to choose someone to help you. Start by picking a class name from the hat or bag, then select a child from that class.
- Ask the child to shake the box. Is there anything inside?
- Take the lid off the box and tell the child to look inside. What or who is there? (The child will see a reflection.)
- Explain that each of us is special - and that anyone could have been chosen to look inside.

Reflection: Close your eyes and think about who you see when you look in a mirror, and remember that you are special. God knows that we are all special.

Worship: 'Every colour under the sun', in *Every Colour under the Sun* (Ward Lock Educational).

Follow-up Assembly:
- Talk about friendships and how friends are special.
- Ask the children to think about one of their friends and why that friend is special.
- Select six children. Ask each one to name the friend they were thinking of, and invite that child to come forward.
- Find out why each friend is special.

NAMES

Focus: God knows everyone by name.

You will need: a book of name meanings; pieces of card (about 24cm x 10cm); felt-tip pens and a Bible.

The Assembly:
- Explain to the children that in the Bible it says that God knows everyone by name.

  > God said, "Don't be afraid: I have saved you and I have called you by your name. You are mine." (Isaiah 43 : 1)

  > The people said "God has forgotten us", but God said, "Can a mother forget her baby? But even if a mother forgets, I will not forget you. I have written your name on my hand." (Isaiah 49 : 14-16)

- We all have names which were given to us when we were babies.
- Ask staff members (warn them first!) if they know how their names were chosen. If they have children, ask them how they chose their names.
- Names have meanings. If you know the meaning of your own name, talk about this.
- Jesus had friends called disciples. If there are children who have the same names as the disciples, ask them to join you. (Remember the feminine versions, for example Philip - Philippa.)
- Write some of the disciples' names on the pieces of card and talk about their meanings.

Reflection: Think of your own name and remember that God knows you by your name.

Worship:
The light of God surrounds me;
The love of God enfolds me;
The power of God protects me;
The presence of God watches over me.
Wherever I am, God is.

Anon

Follow-up Assembly:
Talk about christenings. If possible, have some of the articles associated with christenings: a christening gown, a scallop shell (used to scoop water on to the child's head), baptismal candle and cards.

NEIGHBOURS

Focus: Who is my neighbour?

You will need: a piece of card or paper (60cm long x 12cm wide, folded concertina fashion into 6 x 10cm sections); a pair of scissors; a felt-tip pen; and a large demonstration/display terrace of houses (out of sight).

The Assembly:
- Show the children the piece of paper, folded and unfolded. Fold again and cut to make a small terrace of houses.
- Talk to the children about neighbours. Who is a neighbour?
- Introduce the large terrace of houses, and invite children to come and stand behind the houses. Who is next door to whom?
- Develop the language and vocabulary - next door, next door but one, etc.
- How can we be good neighbours? Make a list of the children's suggestions.
- Neighbours are not just the people who live in the next door house.
- Think about classrooms. Which classes are neighbours?
- Ask each class in turn which class is next to them in school. Which class is their neighbour?
- In the Bible (Luke 10 : 25-37), Jesus said that we should love our neighbour. He meant we should love everyone, because we are all neighbours.

Reflection: Remember we are all neighbours and we should love one another.

Worship: Sing 'When I needed a neighbour', in *Someone's Singing, Lord* (A&C Black).

Follow-up Assembly:
Tell the story of the Good Samaritan (Luke 10 : 25-37). This is an excellent story to act out, and it can be translated into the present, using the idea of a child falling over on the way to school.

THE NEW YEAR

Focus: The cycle of the months marking the end of the old year and beginning of the new year.

You will need: twelve headbands - one for each month of the year; two banners, one reading 'Last year - the old year', and the other reading 'This year - the new year'; the previous year's diary or school log book.

The Assembly:
● This assembly should take place at the very beginning of the spring term.
● Select twelve children to wear the months-of-the-year headbands, and four tall children to be on hand to hold up the banners (two per banner).
● Ask the children what happened during last year. Maybe read from the school log book or diary to remind them.
● Ask the months-of-the-year children to stand up and then ask the whole school to read out the months.
● Talk about saying good-bye to the old year and hello to the new year.
● Ask the banner holders to raise their banners high, and ask the months-of-the-year children to walk, in order, under the old year banner and then under the new year banner.

Reflection: As we say goodbye to the old year and hello to the new year, think about how to make each day a better day in *(name the new year)*.

Worship: Dear Lord Jesus, we have this day only once;
                    before it is gone, help us to do
                    all the good we can,
                    so that this day is not a wasted day.

                                      Stephen Grellet (1773 - 1855)

Follow-up Assembly:
● For this assembly you will need seven headbands (one for each day of the week), and two banners (one reading 'Last week' and the other 'This week').
● Follow the same sequence of discussions and actions, but focus on how each week brings with it the opportunity to make things better.

PANCAKES

Focus: Why do we have pancakes before Lent starts?

You will need: flour, eggs, milk; a large (preferably clear Pyrex) mixing bowl; and a rotary hand beater; if possible, a cooked pancake in a small frying pan. (It may, in some schools, be possible to cook the pancakes during the assembly, but this is not essential.)

The Assembly:
- Describe the background to Pancake Day. Explain how its other name is Shrove Tuesday, and that this is the day before the start of Lent when Christians remember how Jesus spent forty days and forty nights in the wilderness. (Remember to explain terms like 'wilderness' carefully.) He did this partly to prepare himself for his work.
- Because Jesus had no food and not much water during this time, people remembered this by giving up their usual food and eating very little.
- In order to use up their eggs and milk, or to have one last feast, it became the custom to have pancakes.
- Ask one or two children to help, and demonstrate how to make pancakes.
- Explain that pancakes are tossed so that the second side can be cooked. If you have a cooked pancake show the children how to do this.
- If it is not possible to have a cooked pancake, a parent helper could be asked to cook the pancakes and take them round the classes - for tossing and tasting - after the assembly.

Reflection: Remember Jesus' days in the wilderness and how he gave up his usual life to prepare himself for his work.

Worship: Thank you for the world so sweet,
                         Thank you for the food we eat,
                         Thank you for the birds that sing,
                         Thank you, God, for everything.

Follow-up Assembly:
- Remind the children of the reasons for Pancake Day.
- Tell the story of *The Big Pancake* (traditional).

PRECIOUS THINGS

Focus: The really precious things in life.

You will need: two sets of identical objects with one set sprayed gold (use a spray paint that will adhere to non-porous surfaces). Before the assembly, place the ordinary objects on a table, and the gold objects in a box.

The Assembly:
- Begin by telling the children that some people think gold is the most precious thing in the whole world. (Do not ask the children their opinion at this point.)
- Tell them the story of King Midas. As you refer to the objects that the King touched, show them the ordinary object, then show them the identical gold one.

> Thousands of years ago there was a king called Midas. He had been very helpful and he was told that as a reward he could choose anything he liked. He said 'I wish that everything I touch shall be turned into gold'. His wish came true - everything he touched immediately turned into gold. He touched a (hold up object) and it turned into gold (hold up gold replica). This happened many times. Soon he had turned most of the things in his palace into gold. He realized that he could become the richest man in the world, so he decided to hold a great feast to celebrate. When the food arrived he touched it and it too turned into gold, as did everything he tried to drink.

Reflection: What did King Midas realize?

Worship: Dear God, help us to realize what is really precious in our lives.

Assembly ending: Tell the children that King Midas realized how foolish he had been. He was told to go and dip himself in the river. As he did so, the strange power he had to turn things into gold left him. But it is said that as he left the river the sand turned a golden colour, and that is still the colour of sand today.

Follow-up Assembly:
- Show the children the following pairs of objects: a picture of a car and a picture of a baby; a piece of silver jewellery and a jug of water; and a £1 coin and a loaf of bread.
- Ask them which of each pair is the most precious, and why.

PROMISES

Focus: Making and keeping promises.

You will need: a post box (made out of a cardboard carton if necessary); sheets of A4 paper; envelopes (as large as possible, but make sure they can be 'posted'); some felt-tip pens; and your school rules; if possible, a set of classroom rules.

The Assembly:
- Ask the children what they mean by a promise. Do they always keep their promises?
- Our school and classroom rules are promises. Remind the children of your school rules. Can any of the children tell you their classroom rules? (These are usually unique to each class, drawn up by the children.) If possible, discuss a set of classroom rules.
- Select some volunteers to each think of one important promise. Write these on the paper:
            'I promise to ....' (one for each child)
- Ask the children to sign their promises, put the letter in an envelope, seal it and 'post' it.
- Remind all the children that promises are meant to be kept and that it is up to them to do this.
- Leave the post box so that children can make promises after the assembly.

Reflection: God makes promises and he always keeps them. Think about how we should keep the promises that we make.

Worship: Ask the children to sit quietly and make a promise to God which they will keep, with his help.

Follow-up Assembly:
- Remind the children of the story of Noah's Ark (Genesis 6, 7, 8).
- Tell them that after the flood, God made a promise to Noah that there would be seasons so that food would grow and could be harvested (Genesis 8 : 20-22).

50

REMEMBERING

Focus: It is easy to forget things. Sometimes special symbols help us to remember important events.

You will need: a collection of at least ten large objects that will easily be seen by all the children (cover the objects with a cloth before the assembly); a one-minute sand timer; a large piece of paper clipped to a board or easel; and a large felt-tip pen.

The Assembly:
- Ask all the children if they have good memories.
- Explain how to play 'Kim's game', and select two volunteers to take part.
- Remove the cloth and allow one minute for looking at the objects before covering them again.
- Find out how many objects the two volunteers can remember. (This particular game is not competitive.) Write the answers down for all to see.
- Remove the cloth and compare the list of remembered objects with the real ones. Find out if any were forgotten, and discuss how easy it is to forget things.
- Tell the children that some things should not be forgotten, and ask them what they think it is important to remember.

Reflection: One way of remembering others is to pray for them. In our prayers today we are asking God to remember us.

Worship: O Lord, you know how busy
         I shall be this day.
         If I forget you,
         do not forget me.
            Jacob Astley (1579 - 1652)

Follow-up Assembly: See page 71.

See Follow-up Assembly - page 71

SAINT FRANCIS

Focus: Saint Francis, the patron saint of animals. (Saint's day - 4th October)

You will need: a collection of animals and birds. These can be soft toys, ornaments and plastic models that the children bring into the assembly and place on a central table before they sit in their places.

The Assembly:
- Begin by thanking all the children who brought in toys, ornaments and models.
- Explain that these were needed because the assembly is about Saint Francis. Explain that he lived in Italy about 900 years ago. He was a kind and gentle man who helped people and cared for God's creatures.
- Get some volunteers to act out the story of St Francis and the wolf, as you tell it.

> Everyone in the city was scared of the wolf, and they wanted to kill it. St Francis went off alone into the forest to find it. The wolf sprang out at him, snarling and baring its teeth. St Francis asked the wolf not to harm him, but to come with him into the city. At first, the people would not let them through the city gate because they did not trust the wolf. But St Francis talked to them and fed the wolf. The people grew to trust the wolf, and he stayed in the city and became everyone's pet.

Reflection: I am going to read to you a prayer that was first said by St Francis himself. He talks about earth, the sun, the moon and the weather as though they were all part of a big family. Listen carefully.

Worship:
> Praised be my Lord, for our Brother Sun,
> Who caused all day his course to run.
> For our Sister Moon, praised be my Lord,
> By stars in heavenly hosts adored.
> For our Brothers, the Wind, the Cloud and the Air,
> Whose blessings all your creatures share.
> Praised be my Lord for Waters bright,
> For our Brother fire, for warmth and light,
> To Mother Earth, your gifts you send,
> O God, our Father, and our Friend.
>
> St Francis (1181 - 1226)

Follow-up Assembly: See page 71.

SEEING RED AND FEELING BLUE

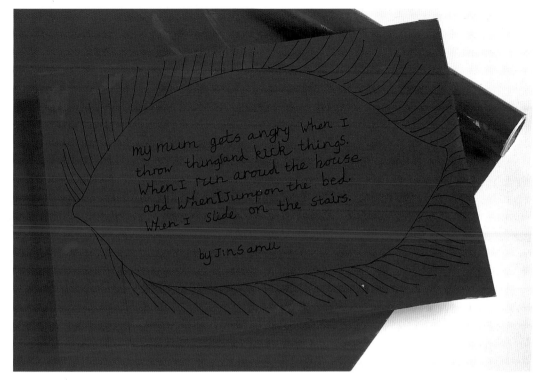

my mum gets angry when I
throw things and kick things.
When I run around the house
and when I jump on the bed,
When I slide on the stairs.

by Jin Samu

Classroom follow-up work

Focus: Understanding the types of behaviour that anger or sadden people; realizing how our actions affect others; and the idea of forgiveness.

You will need: a sheet of red cellophane.

The Assembly:
● Invite a volunteer to come and look through the cellophane. Ask the volunteer to describe to the other children what everything looks like.
● Explain that sometimes people 'see red' even when they are not looking through Cellophane.
● Find out if anyone knows what it means 'to see red'.
● Ask the children if their mothers or fathers ever get angry with them.
● Invite some volunteers to explain what they do that makes their parents angry.
● Discuss how this could be avoided, and what they could do or say to show they are sorry.

Reflection: Think about what you do that makes your mother or father angry. What could you do to stop this happening?

Worship: Forgive us the wrongs we have done,
                        as we forgive the wrongs that have been done to us.
                                          Matthew 6 : 12

Follow-up Assembly:
● Talk about the other colours that are associated with feelings, for example,
            turning white as a sheet (with fear)
            turning green with envy
            going pink with embarrassment
            feeling blue
● Explain that the 'blues' is a type of music that came from the U.S.A. It was sung when African-American people felt sad or troubled.
● Play some blues music.
● Discuss with the children what others do that makes them feel sad, and how they respond if someone deliberately tries to upset them. Are they able to forgive and forget?

SHEEP

Focus: In the Bible it says that Jesus is like a shepherd, and we are his sheep.

You will need: models of sheep (see photograph); a large sheet of paper and felt-tip pens; if possible, a shepherd's crook. Put a model of a sheep at the back of the hall, but where it can be reached. Put the rest of the sheep on the assembly table.

Follow-up Assembly - see below

The Assembly:
- Begin by showing the children how to tally.
- Select a child to be the shepherd. Ask the shepherd to count the sheep.
- Tally up to 99 - in fives - a sheep is missing because there should be 100.
- The 'shepherd' goes to look for the sheep, brings it back and places it on the table.
- The 'shepherd' completes the tallying.
- Explain that Jesus told this story about the shepherd to his followers to show how God cares for everyone (The lost sheep, Matthew 18 : 10-14).

Reflection: Think about how a shepherd looks after his sheep. Why do you think Jesus said 'I am the good shepherd?'

Worship: The King of love my shepherd is,
                 Whose goodness faileth never;
                 I nothing lack if I am his
                 And he is mine for ever.

                 Henry Williams Baker (1821 - 1877)

Follow-up Assembly:
- The shepherd in the story of the lost sheep made sure all the sheep were safe. When one went missing, he looked until he found it.
- What else does a good shepherd do?
- Write a list of the children's suggestions. This could be written on a cut-out sheep shape (see photograph above).
- How does God look after us?

SHOES

Classroom follow-up work

Focus: What is meant by 'stepping into someone else's shoes'?

You will need: two pairs of adult footwear that are associated with different sports or jobs, for example, tennis shoes, ballet shoes, wellington boots, flippers, workman's boots with steel toe caps; one pair of children's shoes.

The Assembly:
- Set out the pairs of adult footwear.
- Ask for a volunteer to come and 'step into someone else's shoes'.
- Ask the volunteer to imagine s/he is the owner of the footwear.
- Discuss with the rest of the children who the footwear might belong to, and what it would be worn for.
- Repeat with another volunteer and the other footwear.
- Ask the volunteers if they enjoyed pretending to be someone else.
- Now produce the pair of children's shoes.
- Explain that these belong to a child who has no friends and nobody to play with at playtimes.

Reflection: Imagine that you are standing in these shoes. How do you feel? If you saw someone standing alone in the playground, what would you do?

Worship: How can I see another's sadness,
And not be sad too?
How can I see another's pain,
And not seek to help.
Adapted from the words of William Blake (1757 - 1827)

Follow-up Assembly:
- Ask for a volunteer to wear some foam ear plugs. Continue the assembly by reminding the children about what it is like to step into someone else's shoes.
- Get the child to remove the earplugs and to share with the other children what it was like being nearly deaf.
- Repeat this with another volunteer - this time using a blindfold instead of earplugs.
- Discuss ways in which we can help the deaf and the blind.

What will grow from the pip ?

Focus: New life and the cycle which brings about new life.

You will need: a branch of apple blossom (or a small apple tree in a pot); a 2D apple made of card which is in two layers; an apple tree drawn on folded card (see photograph).

The Assembly:
- Ask the children if anyone has brought an apple to school today.
- What is an apple like inside?
- As soon as a child mentions the pips, ask a volunteer to 'peel' the large apple.
- Ask the volunteer to point to the pips.
- Why are there pips inside the apple? What happens to the pips?
- Demonstrate using the folded card.
- What would the tree look like at this time of the year? After discussion, show children the blossom.
- Tell the children that farmers check their trees at this time of year. If there is no blossom in the spring, there will be no fruit in the autumn.

Reflection: Remember that new life depends on the yearly cycle. God made a promise that there would always be Spring - and new life.

Worship: The year's at the Spring;
                  And day's at the morn;
                  Morning's at seven;
                  The hillside's dew-pearled;
                  The lark's on the wing;
                  The snail's on the thorn;
                  God's in his heaven -
                  All's right with the world!

from 'Pippa Passes', Pt 1, by Robert Browning (1812 - 1889)

Follow-up Assembly:
- Plan a dance sequence.
- Begin with some children as seeds hidden under the 'earth' (blankets or duvet).
- Introduce a child as the sun, whose presence makes the 'seeds' begin to grow.

STARS

A suggested display for after the assembly

Focus: How can we all be stars?

You will need: a display board; drawing pins; a large hexagram drawn on white card; scissors; a felt-tip pen and a sheet of paper.

The Assembly:
- Ask the children for ideas about what a star is.
- Explain that a 'star' can also be a person who is special and stands out in the crowd like a star in the sky. We can all be 'stars'.
- Show the children the hexagram, and explain that together you are going to make a star.
- Cut the hexagram into a hexagon and six triangles.
- Brainstorm ideas of what makes someone a star. Draw out qualities such as *caring, hard-working, friendly, happy, smiling,* etc. Write a list.
- Select a child to help you. Write the child's name on the hexagon, then ask him/her to choose six things from the list that would make him/her into a star. Write these on the triangles and assemble to make a hexagram on a display board.
- Explain that this is the child's 'star' and s/he is going to try to be all of these things.
- Each child could make a star for a display, with a photograph in the centre.

Reflection: Think of the things which would make you a star and a very special person.

Worship: Sing 'God, who put the stars in space', in *Someone's Singing, Lord* (A&C Black).

Follow-up Assembly:
- You will need some cut-out stars.
- Talk about stars of screen and stage. See if children know the names of any famous stars.
- Explain that pop stars are good at singing, and film stars are good at acting.
- Select children to tell you what they themselves are good at doing. Write the child's name on a star, together with 'I am good at ....'.

SUKKOT

We made a model of a sukkah.

Focus: Remembering the days the Israelites spent in the wilderness, and how God blesses us with harvest.

You will need: a table turned upside-down (tape four canes to the legs to form a framework - see photograph); corrugated card; some branches; crêpe paper streamers; real or artificial fruit.

The Assembly:
* Begin by explaining that the Israelites had escaped from captivity and were to spend many years wandering in the desert.
* Tell the children about Sukkot:

    The Jewish people remember the years of wandering by celebrating a festival called Sukkot, which lasts for eight days. During their time of wandering, they built huts in which they lived called *sukkah* and, to remember this, huts are built in gardens or in the synagogue, where Jewish people worship. The huts are decorated with flowers and fruit, and the sky can be seen through the roof. God looked after the Jewish people and provided food, and this is what is celebrated at Sukkot.

* Invite children to help you decorate the model of the sukkah - use crêpe and tissue paper streamers, and the fruit.
* Explain that Jewish people eat in their sukkah. Put a small table and chair inside the model of the sukkah to illustrate this.

Reflection: Think about how Sukkot is a time of rejoicing and thanksgiving for the Jewish people because of all that God provides.

Worship: Prayer is for the soul, what food is for the body.
The blessing of one prayer lasts until the next,
Just as the strength gained from one meal lasts until the one after.
                                        (a Jewish prayer)

Follow-up Assembly:
* Remind the children of the festival of Sukkot.
* Display fruit and vegetables around the model sukkah.
* Explain that Jewish people thank God for the harvest at this time.

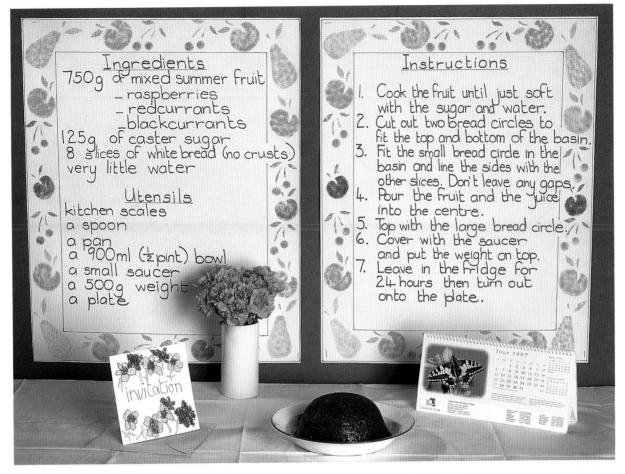

Ingredients
750g of mixed summer fruit
 − raspberries
 − redcurrants
 − blackcurrants
125g of caster sugar
8 slices of white bread (no crusts)
very little water

Utensils
kitchen scales
a spoon
a pan
a 900ml (½ pint) bowl
a small saucer
a 500g weight
a plate

Instructions
1. Cook the fruit until just soft with the sugar and water.
2. Cut out two bread circles to fit the top and bottom of the basin.
3. Fit the small bread circle in the basin and line the sides with the other slices. Don't leave any gaps.
4. Pour the fruit and the juice into the centre.
5. Top with the large bread circle.
6. Cover with the saucer and put the weight on top.
7. Leave in the fridge for 24 hours then turn out onto the plate.

Focus: Summer is the season for fresh fruits. Mark the occasion by making a summer pudding, and invite a visitor to the follow-up assembly to share the fruits of summer.

You will need: two sheets of A1 card: one listing the ingredients and utensils, and the other detailing the recipe (see photograph); the ingredients and utensils listed. You will need to pre-prepare stages 1 and 2 of the recipe before the assembly. Remember to save a few uncooked fruits to show the children.

The Assembly:
- Ask for two volunteers to hold up the cards, and ask other children to read the lists of ingredients and utensils.
- Show these to the children.
- Read out stages 1 and 2 of the recipe and explain that you did these before the assembly.
- Invite some volunteers to taste the uncooked fruits, and to describe the taste and texture.
- Select more helpers to help you complete the recipe.

Reflection: Think about your favourite fruit. Think about sharing it with others.

Worship: Make us ever eager, Lord, to share the good things that we have.
John Hunter (1849 - 1917)

Follow-up Assembly:
- Cover a table with a cloth and put out three bowls and three spoons.
- Invite a visitor (governor, parent or community leader) to join the assembly, having first got his/her agreement to do a 'blindfold tasting'.
- Place the summer pudding on the table and serve the blindfolded visitor.
- Encourage the visitor to describe the taste and texture of the food.
- Having removed the blindfold, ask the visitor to select two children to sample the pudding.
- Finally, draw a class name from a hat to find out which class can finish off the pudding!

SUNSHINE

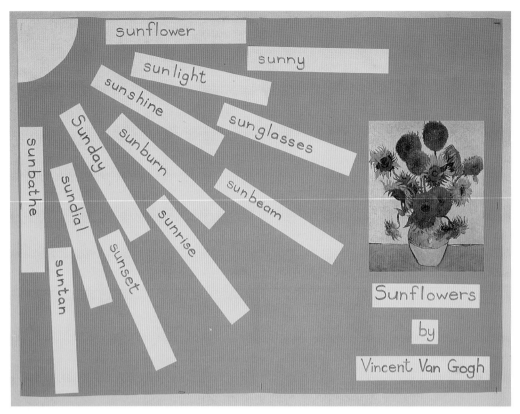

A suggested display for after the assembly

Focus: We need the sun, but we must remember it is strong and it can be dangerous.

You will need: a print of Van Gogh's 'Sunflowers'; strips of yellow card (approx. 30cm x 5cm, i.e. quarter A4 lengthwise); a thick felt-tip pen; and a quarter circle of yellow card to complete the display (optional).

The Assembly:
- Show the children the print of Van Gogh's 'Sunflowers'.
- Ask them to think of other words that begin with the prefix *sun*.
- Write down each suggestion on a strip of card, and get the child who suggested the word to hold it up.
- Count the number of 'sun' words that have been suggested.
- Find out if the children know why the sun is so important for life on earth.
- Discuss the importance of the sun as a source of both light and warmth.

Reflection: Imagine a world without any sunshine. Now think about how we need the sun in our lives.

Worship: Sing 'The golden cockerel' in *Someone's Singing, Lord* (A&C Black).

Follow-up Assembly:
- Remind the children that although the sun is essential for life on earth it can be dangerous.
- Discuss the different ways in which they can protect themselves from the sun; for example, hat, sunscreen, etc.
- Tell them the Aesop's fable about the north wind and the sun. Which was stronger?
- Select three children to act it out: one as the man wearing a cloak; another as the sun holding a sun mask; and the third as the wind holding a cloud mask.

THANKSGIVING

A suggested display for after the assembly

Focus: Thanksgiving is celebrated in the USA on the fourth Thursday in November. It is a time when American families remember how the Pilgrim Fathers gave thanks for their survival during those first winters in their new land.

You will need: a basket of foods that originated in the Americas, for example, pumpkin, squash, sweetcorn, 'Jerusalem' artichokes; labels for each food item; a tape or CD of some Native American music; if possible, a flag from the USA; and a picture of the Pilgrim Fathers.

The Assembly:
- Tell the children the story of the Pilgrim Fathers.

  > Nearly 400 years ago, some people left England because they were not allowed to pray to God in the way they wanted. They sailed to America. When they arrived they did not have enough to eat, especially during the long, cold winter. They were helped by the local people - the Native Americans - who gave them food and told them what was safe to eat.
- Play the music as you select volunteers to unpack the basket. Get the helpers to show each item of food. Explain how all these foods were first grown in America.
- Select additional helpers to match each label to the food items.
- Tell the children that the Pilgrim Fathers had a special meal to say thank you to God.

Reflection: What is good in your life? What do you want to thank God for?

Worship: Thou who has given so much to me
                  Give me one more thing, a grateful heart.
                              George Herbert (1593 - 1632)

Follow-up Assembly:
- String a washing line across the hall. Have ready some clothes pegs, some strips of sugar paper (approx 10cm x 60cm) and a large felt-tip pen.
- Discuss with the children how easy it is, when we are fed up, to forget all the good things in our lives. Ask the children to name the good things in their lives.
- As they give examples, write each down on a strip of paper and secure it on the line with a peg.
- At the end of the assembly, invite the children to 'count their blessings'.

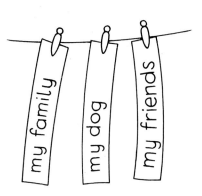

TOYS

Focus: Toys are made from a variety of materials. As a boy, Jesus probably played with wooden toys. Most children have a favourite toy which is very special.

You will need: a bag containing a selection of wooden toys (try to include balsa models made by the children); four blindfolds; a soft toy, a plastic toy and a metallic toy.

The Assembly:
- Show the children the toy bag but not its contents.
- Select four volunteers to be blindfolded and hand each one a different toy made from a different material (fabric, plastic, metal and wood).
- Ask each volunteer if s/he knows what the toy is made of.
- Untie the blindfolds and let the helpers examine their toys to see if their guesses were correct.
- Tell the children about the early life of Jesus: how he lived in Nazareth with his brothers and sisters; and how his father was a carpenter.
- Find out if the children know what a carpenter does.
- Explain how some people think Joseph may have made small wooden toys for Jesus to play with.
- Select additional children to take the remaining wooden toys out of the bag, talking about each one as they do so.

Reflection: Think about the toys you have at home. Which is your favourite? Close your eyes and imagine it. Think about what makes it so special.

Worship: Thank you God for all our toys,
                      For new ones
                      And old favourites too.
                      May we find joy in sharing them with others.

Follow-up Assembly
- On the day before the assembly, ask three children each to bring in a favourite toy.
- Ask each child to show the toy and explain why it is a favourite.
- Find out how they would feel if these toys got lost or broken.
- Read a story about a lost toy, for example, *Dogger*, by Shirley Hughes (Little Greats, Random Century).

VEGETABLES

Focus: Autumn is the season when farmers and gardeners gather most of their vegetables to store for the cold winter months.

You will need: a large tin of vegetable soup; a collection of vegetables needed to make vegetable soup (in a large basket); labels of the vegetable names; if possible, a large tureen and ladle. (This is suitable for a class assembly, especially if a class actually has made soup in the classroom.)

The Assembly:
● Show the children the tin of vegetable soup.
● Ask them what might go in to vegetable soup.
● If a class has made vegetable soup, ask them to help.
● Use the children's suggestions to make a list of ingredients.
● Ask volunteers to come out and take vegetables out of the basket - one for each child. Ask them to describe their vegetable and find its label. Where does it grow? What part of the plant is it (stem, leaf, seed, root)?
● What happens to vegetables after the farmers and gardeners have harvested them? Talk about storing, canning, freezing, etc.

Reflection: Thank God for the harvest of vegetables.

Worship: Sing 'Paint-box' in *Harlequin* (A&C Black).

Follow-up Assembly:
Remind the children of vegetable harvest. Tell the story of *The Enormous Turnip* (traditional).

WATER

Other uses
swimming
car washes
cleaning teeth
flushing the toilet
fountains
fish tanks

A suggested display for after the assembly

Focus: We use water every day. It is a precious gift.

You will need: all the objects shown in the photograph above (cover these with a cloth before the assembly); a large piece of sugar paper clipped to an easel or board; and a thick felt-tip pen.

The Assembly
- Ask the children what we use water for. If a suggestion matches an object under the cloth, ask the child who had the idea to come to the front and to remember his suggestion until later.
- Any additional suggestions that do not match the objects can be written down on the sugar paper.
- As soon as enough suggestions have been generated, remove the cloth.
- Ask each child to hold up the object that matches his or her suggestion.

Reflection: Imagine your life if there was little or no water.

Worship: Thank you, God, for water and its many uses.

Follow-up Assembly
You will need 10 empty plastic buckets (with a volunteer sitting beside each one), an empty washing up bowl and a bucket of water. Pour the water into the bowl to show how much water is used when washing up. Ask the children how much water is used for showering, bathing and using the washing machine. Get the volunteers to hold up buckets to show the amounts used. If the children are familiar with lawn sprinklers, explain how one sprinkler uses the equivalent of 90 buckets in one hour.

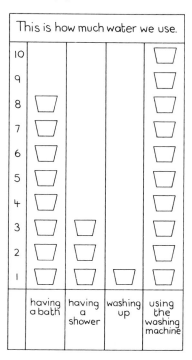

This is how much water we use.

	having a bath	having a shower	washing up	using the washing machine
10				▭
9				▭
8	▭			▭
7	▭			▭
6	▭			▭
5	▭			▭
4	▭			▭
3	▭	▭		▭
2	▭	▭		▭
1	▭	▭	▭	▭

WEAVING

We have woven a very special fabric for our school.

Madras check | binca
hessian | gingham

love
smile
trust
understand
think
listen
give
help
share
care

a woven rug from Mexico

Focus: A special fabric made with woven words.

You will need: samples of woven fabrics (for example, tartan, binca, hessian, gingham, etc.); a wooden drawing board (approx. 60cm x 40cm); ten drawing pins; some string or wool; and strips of card (50cm x 5cm) on which are written: *care, share, help, give, listen, think, understand, trust, smile* and *love.* Pre-prepare the drawing board with the drawing pins and wool, but do not weave in the strips of card.

The Assembly:
- Show the children a range of different woven materials. Find out if anyone has done some weaving and talk about how the threads go under and over, under and over, etc.
- Explain that you want to weave a special fabric for the school, but you will need some help.
- Show the children the pre-prepared board.
- Choose a volunteer to come out. Ask him/her to select a strip of card, read the word on it and then weave it onto the board starting at the base.
- Repeat with different children for the remaining strips.

Reflection: Think about the words we have woven, and what they mean.

Worship: Dear God,
                    Help us to weave a special fabric for our school.
                    Help us to care, share, help, give, listen, think,
                    understand, trust, smile and love,
                    so that together we can make our school a happier place.

Follow-up Assembly:
- Pre-prepare a board as before, and have ten strips of card cut ready.
- Tell the children that you are going to weave, with their help, a fabric of their achievements.
- Select a child to tell you one thing that s/he can do and is proud of (for example, *I can tie my shoe-laces; I can count to 100*).
- Write the achievement on a strip of card and ask the child to weave it on to the board.
- Repeat with additional children.
(In a class assembly, individual children could make their own achievement mats and read them out.)

WHY?

OUR SCHOOL BEHAVIOUR CODE

1. We come to school to learn.

2. We listen to others.

3. We care for others.

4. We keep safe.

5. We look after our school and everything in it.

6. We only bring to school what we need.

Focus: Understanding the school's behaviour code.

You will need: a slip of paper on which is written the joke: *Which letter of the alphabet asks a question?*; and two glove puppets in a box (any creatures or characters will do).

The Assembly:
- Begin the assembly by asking a volunteer to come and read the joke that is written on the slip of paper.
- Find out if anyone knows the answer ('Y').
- Tell the children you have a friend who is always asking the question 'Why?' and another friend who usually knows the answers.
- Put on one of the glove puppets and introduce the character to the children.
- Get your puppet to ask the children a question about your school's behaviour code. For example, Why must we listen to others?
- Select a child who is volunteering to answer to come up, put on the second glove puppet, introduce the character and tell everyone the answer.
- Continue wearing your glove puppet and continue asking further questions about the behaviour code.
- Select different volunteers to wear the other puppet and to give the answers.

Reflection: Which rule do you find the most difficult to keep? Think about why we have that rule, and how it helps our school to be a better place.

Worship:

May I be happy
May I be peaceful
May I be free

May my friends be happy
May my friends be peaceful
May my friends be free.

Words from a Buddhist Prayer

(It would not be appropriate to end with "Amen".)

Follow-up Assembly:
- Use the two puppets and the same question and answer format to explore playground behaviour.
- Discuss ways in which the children can play happily and safely.

THE WIDER WORLD

Focus: A child's place in the wider world.

You will need: an envelope made from the largest square of paper that you have available; an easel or board; a thick felt-tip pen; an individual portrait and a class photograph of a selected child; a picture of the school; maps of - the immediate locality, the wider area, the U.K., Europe and the world; pictures of the solar system and the universe. These props need to be arranged in order before the assembly.

The Assembly:
- Begin by showing the children the large envelope and clip it to the easel or board.
- Introduce the child that you have chosen. Explain that you are going to write the child's name and the school address on the envelope, so that if it got posted from 'far, far away', then it would be sure to arrive at the school.
- Write the child's name on the envelope while the child shows his/her portrait to the other children.
- Ask the children which class the child belongs to, then select the child who answers to show the class photograph as you write the next line of the address.
- As you write each line of the address, select helpers to hold up the appropriate map or picture.
- Read through the full address together.

Adelaide Robinson,
Class 1B,
 Southfield Primary School,
 Southfield Road,
  London W4 1BD,
  England,
   Europe,
    The World,
     The Solar System,
      The Universe.

Reflection: Think about your place in the world.

Worship: Sing 'He's got the whole world in his hands', in *Every Colour under the Sun* (Ward Lock Educational).

Follow-up Assembly: See page 71.

Focus: Winter days

You will need: the poem 'The North Wind doth Blow'; and some children; if possible, pictures of a robin, a swallow, a dormouse, a bee (or beehive).

The Assembly:
- Read the poem 'The North Wind doth Blow'.
- Talk about each verse in turn, using the pictures to illustrate your narrative.
- Discuss the issues raised. How can we help birds survive the cold weather (food, water, bird table)?
- Where do migrating birds go? What hazards might they face on their journey?
- Which animals hibernate? Think about the environmental aspects (destruction of habitats, etc.).
- Do we see bees in the winter? Where are they?
- How do we keep warm on cold winter days?

Reflection: Think about animals in the cold weather. Remember to feed them and give them water.

Worship: 'Little Birds in Winter Time', in *Someone's Singing, Lord* (A&C Black).

Follow-up Assembly:
You will need: a warm coat, scarf, hat, gloves, insulated flask, hot water bottle.
- Remind the children about how we keep warm in winter.
- What do we wear?
- What do we eat and drink?
- How can we make sure that elderly people who live alone can manage to keep warm in winter?
- Are there any other ways that we can help, for example, clearing snow from paths, doing shopping, etc.

WISHING AND WANTING

Focus: We are often prevented from appreciating what we have by spending time wanting things that we have not got.

You will need: four model trees made from: four pieces of A4 card, folded and cut as shown; some gold and silver paper; some dull green crêpe paper; some coloured cellophane. Cut fringes as shown, glue the fringes on to each model tree, starting at the base, and work upwards. Place the model trees in a box.

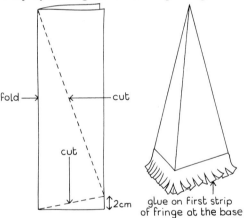

The Assembly:
Tell the story of the fir tree, taking each model tree out of the box at the appropriate point in the story:

> Once upon a time there was a green fir tree who was very unhappy. He did not like his dull, dark green leaves, and he thought he would be happy if only he had different leaves. Suddenly his wish came true and he had beautiful brightly coloured glass leaves. But these got broken when the wind blew. So then he wished for silver leaves and again his wish came true. But these leaves tarnished in the rain. Next he wished for gold leaves and again his wish came true. But these leaves were stolen from his branches. Finally, the fir tree realised that he had been better off with his dark evergreen leaves. This last wish came true and he began to realise that maybe life was not so bad after all!

Reflection: Have you ever felt like that fir tree? Have you really wanted something, then, having got it, realised that it was not so important after all?

Worship: Waking up each morning, I will smile.
A new day will be before me.
I will try to live fully in each moment.

(Adapted from the words of Thich Nhat Hanh)

Follow-up Assembly: See page 71.

Follow-up Assemblies

Christmas Countdown
In each subsequent assembly, get the selected children to wear their headbands and invite additional children to join them as the month progresses. This "countdown to Christmas" can precede the telling of each section of the Christmas story or the reading of other seasonal tales. Remember to add and light an additional floating candle each week, saving the white one until the final assembly of the term. Tell the children about what each candle symbolizes:

The First candle is for the coming of Christ.
The Second candle is for God's promise.
The Third candle is for the birth of John the Baptist.

The Fourth candle is for Mary, mother of Jesus.
The Fifth candle is for the birth of Jesus.

Christmas Evergreens
- Begin by reminding the children about the legend of the rosemary bush. Find out if they remember any other special smells or scents at Christmas time.
- Select three volunteers to help make a seasonal pot pourri.
- One helper hammers some cinnamon sticks into small pieces; another breaks up pieces of dried orange rind into smaller pieces; and the third mixes these ingredients with cloves in a bowl.
- Invite a fourth child to come and smell the mixture.

Divali
Show the children a pearl-type necklace. Tell them about the Indian queen who was given such a necklace but who had it stolen by a crow. Tell how a poor woman found it but refused the reward that the king had offered. The only thing that the old woman wanted was for the king to forbid anyone but her to light the divas for Divali. This was done, and when Lakshmi visited it was very dark. The goddess could only see divas shining from one home, and that was the home of the old woman. So the old woman received Lakshmi's blessings that year.

Easter
- You will need a cross made from cube-shaped tissue boxes (see line drawing) and a basket containing seven objects associated with Jesus or Easter (for example, a hot cross bun, an egg, bread, a candle; models of a fish, sheep or donkey; a stone to symbolize the one from the tomb).
- Invite a volunteer to take an object from the basket. Discuss its significance before placing it in the cross.
- Select further volunteers to select objects.
- Remember to highlight the symbolism of new life.

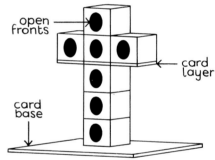

Eid-ul-Fitr
- Make some raita - a dish which some Muslim families eat at Eid-ul-Fitr.

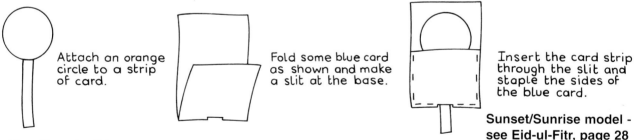

Attach an orange circle to a strip of card.

Fold some blue card as shown and make a slit at the base.

Insert the card strip through the slit and staple the sides of the blue card.

Sunset/Sunrise model - see Eid-ul-Fitr, page 28

- You will need a dish, a grater, two teaspoons, one finely chopped onion, 500ml natural yoghurt, half a cucumber (grated), some cumin seeds and some paprika.
- Invite further volunteers to add to the remaining ingredients, measuring out a quarter teaspoon of cumin seeds and the same quantity of paprika.
- Mix the ingredients and invite some more volunteers to taste the raita.

Guru Nanak's birthday
Show the children the picture of Guru Nanak and tell the story of his birth:
When Guru Nanak was born, the nurse who came to tell his father looked very worried. She said that she had never seen such a baby before. He did not cry like other babies, he simply smiled and a light shone around his head like a star. These things worried the father too, so he sent for the priest. But the priest told him that he was a lucky man. He said that the baby would grow up and become a king or a teacher. When Guru Nanak's sister Bibi Nanaki heard this, she said that the baby would not be king but a teacher. She said he would be a friend to all, and that people would remember him for a very long time. They would call him the Guru.

Homes

Tell the story of the four friends who swapped homes: Once there were four friends - a bird, a rabbit, a pig and an elephant. The bird lived in a nest high up in a tree. The rabbit lived in a burrow under the ground. The pig lived in a sty with the other pigs. The elephant lived alone in the elephant house at the zoo. One day they decided to swap homes. The bird was tired of the tree and rabbit fancied a home with a view, so they swapped places. The pig was tired of living with others, and the elephant was fed up with being alone, so they swapped too. The rabbit found it difficult to climb up the tree and nearly fell out of the nest. The bird found the burrow dark and cramped. The elephant could not fit in the sty, and had to spend the night sleeping on the doorstep. The pig missed his family and was scared being all alone in the elephant's huge house. The next morning they were all very tired and rather miserable, so they decided to swap back. They all realised that there is no place like home.

Music

The format of the assembly (on page 43) can be adapted for other countries provided that you have some music, a collection of artefacts and some pictures or photographs. You will also need to incorporate some sort of practical demonstration. (For example, for Jamaica - make a tropical fruit salad; for Greece - marinade olives and fresh herbs.)

Remembering

• Show the children a Remembrance Day poppy and find out if they know what it is and what it is for. (See photograph on page 51.)
• Discuss how the poppy reminds us of all the people who were hurt or killed during the wars.
• Explain that we think about these people on Remembrance Day.
• Tell the children how World War I stopped at 11 o'clock in the morning on 11th November, which is the eleventh month of the year. Explain how we remember that moment by standing in silence.
• Ask the children to stand in silence just as many grown-ups do.

Saint Francis

• Begin the assembly by cutting some crêpe paper to make a fishing net (see page 30), and by cutting some sugar paper to make a large fish.
• Select a volunteer to be the fisherman and to hold the net containing the fish.
• Select another volunteer to be St Francis who, when given the fish by the fisherman, immediately puts it back in the water.
• Discuss with the children how the fisherman might have felt, and why St Francis did what he did.

The Wider World

• Pre-prepare 20 strips of card (approx 30cm x 10cm - i.e. A4 halved lengthwise).
• Place the globe in a central position.
• Discuss the fact that the children live in the United Kingdom. Ask them if they know the names of any other countries. Write each correct suggestion on a strip of card and get the child who named the country to hold it up. These children should make a circle around the globe.
• When the circle is complete, end the assembly by singing 'He's got the whole world in his hands'.

Wishing and Wanting

Dress a child up as a penguin. Tell the story of a penguin who lived in the Antarctic but who was always complaining about the cold. Tell how he swam north to warmer water but when he reached the tropical island of his dreams, he began complaining about the heat!
(This story could be expanded for a class assembly by dressing additional children up as 'satisfied' penguins. Other children could be islanders who welcome the wandering penguin with gifts of tropical fruit and garlands.)

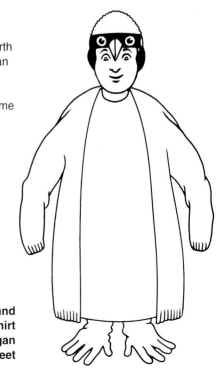

Black woolly hat with headband
Large T-shirt
Adult's black cardigan
Rubber gloves on feet

For details of further Belair publications,
please write to Libby Masters,
BELAIR PUBLICATIONS LIMITED,
Albert House, Apex Business Centre,
Boscombe Road, Dunstable, LU5 4RL.

For sales and distribution in North America and South America,
INCENTIVE PUBLICATIONS,
3835 Cleghorn Avenue, Nashville, Tn 37215,
USA.

For sales and distribution in Australia,
EDUCATIONAL SUPPLIES PTY LTD,
8 Cross Street, Brookvale, NSW 2100,
Australia.

For sales and distribution (in other territories),
FOLENS PUBLISHERS,
Albert House, Apex Business Centre,
Boscombe Road, Dunstable, LU5 4RL,
United Kingdom.
Email: folens@folens.com